Home Repairs

& Improvements

Albert Jackson and David Day

Hearst Books
A Division of Sterling Publishing Co., Inc.
New York

Popular Mechanics
Steve Willson, U.S. Project Editor
Tom Klenck, U.S. Art Director

Created, edited, and designed by Inklink
Concept, editorial, design and art direction: Simon Jennings
Text: Albert Jackson and David Day
Design: Alan Marshall
Illustrations: David Day, Robin Harris, Brian Craker, Michael Parr, Brian Sayers
Photographs: Paul Chave, Peter Higgins, Simon Jennings, Albert Jackson

Hearst Books
Project editor: Joseph Gonzalez

Library of Congress Cataloging-in-Publication Data

Jackson, Albert, 1943-
  Popular mechanics : home repairs & improvements / Albert Jackson and David Day.
    p. cm.
  Includes bibliographical references and index.
  ISBN-13: 978-1-58816-530-5 (alk. paper)
  ISBN-10: 1-58816-530-2 (alk. paper)
  1. Dwellings--Maintenance and repair--Amateurs' manuals.
I. Day, David, 1944- II. Popular Mechanics Press. III. Title.
  TH4817.3.J34 2006
  643'.7--dc22
                                        2006001724

10 9 8 7 6 5 4 3 2 1

Published by Hearst Books
A Division of Sterling Publishing Co., Inc.
387 Park Avenue South
New York, NY 10016

Popular Mechanics and Hearst Books are trademarks of Hearst Communications, Inc.

www.popularmechanics.com

For information about custom editions, special sales, premium and corporate purchases, please contact Sterling Special Sales Department at 800-805-5489 or specialsales@sterlingpub.com.

Distributed in Canada by Sterling Publishing
c/o Canadian Manda Group, 165 Dufferin Street
Toronto, Ontario, Canada M6K 3H6

Printed in China

Sterling ISBN-13: 978-1-58816-530-5
        ISBN-10: 1-58816-530-2

Contents

Wood-framed house

Wood is the predominant material used in residential construction for both structural and finish applications. While there are several approaches to framing a structure with wood—including traditional post-and-beam framing and balloon framing—the platform framing system shown here is the most common approach.

Foundations

The foundations for frame houses are generally either poured concrete or concrete block. Poured concrete footings should be installed under all foundation walls.

Floor construction

In platform framing, the first-floor structure is fastened to sill plates that rest on top of the foundation walls. The basic floor structure is made with 2-inch-thick joists. The ends of the joists are joined to the rim or band joists, and cross-bracing (often called bridging) is nailed between the joists to prevent them from twisting. When openings occur in the joist layout for stairways, or other passages through the plane of the floor, double headers and double joists are installed around the perimeter of the opening for extra strength. Subflooring and finished flooring are installed over the joists.

Wall construction

The walls of a wood-frame house are ordinarily built by nailing the ends of studs to horizontal members called top and bottom plates. The walls are lifted and nailed to the floor. All the loadbearing walls have a double top plate, and usually the interior partitions do too. Where door and window openings occur, headers are installed in the wall to support the weight above each opening. The outside surface of all exterior walls is covered with sheathing, usually some type of manufactured panel.

Roof structure

A traditional roof calls for rafters that rest on top of the house walls and are joined together with a ridge board at the peak. The roof deck is formed by nailing sheathing (usually manufactured panels) over the top edge of the rafters, and then covering the sheathing with asphalt felt and the roofing material: asphalt or wood shingles, slate, or clay tiles.

Foundations
The foundations carry the whole weight of the house. The type, size, and depth are determined largely by the loadbearing properties of the subsoil and by the frost depth in your area.

Wall foundation
A continuous concrete or block wall resting on top of a concrete footing.

Slab foundation
Houses without basements or crawlspaces may have this type of foundation. In cold climates the footings must be set below the frost line.

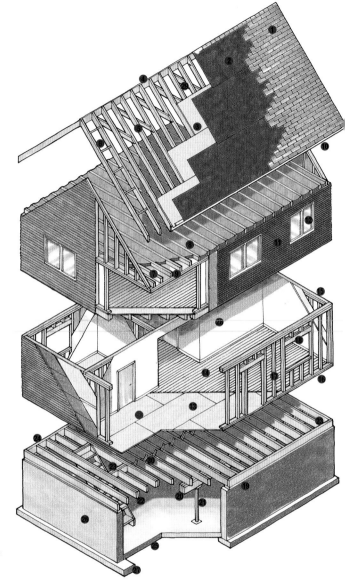

TYPICAL COMPONENTS OF A WOOD-FRAMED HOUSE

1 Asphalt shingles	12 Window unit	23 Double joist header
2 Asphalt felt	13 Subflooring	24 Rim or band joist
3 Sheathing	14 Finish flooring	25 Concrete slab
4 Ridge board	15 Double top plate	26 Foundation wall
5 Rafters	16 Bottom plate	27 Footing
6 Lookouts	17 Stud	28 Loadbearing
7 Ceiling joists	18 Header	partition
8 Insulation	19 Sill plate	29 Collar tie
9 Vapor barrier	20 Girder or beam	30 Cross-bracing
10 Fascia	21 Column	
11 Siding	22 Double joist	

Brick houses tend to follow traditional styles and methods of construction. The brickwork gives the building character and is the main structural element. If you have to repair and renovate your home, it is useful to understand the basic principles of its construction.

Foundation

Brick houses generally have a deep foundation made of concrete block or poured concrete. In older houses, stone or brick may have been used for the foundation.

Wall structure

Cavity wall construction is used to build the perimeter walls of most brick houses. Each wall is constructed of an inner and outer leaf separated by an airspace. The two leaves are braced together with metal or brick ties. A flashing just above the finished grade keeps ground moisture from migrating up the walls. Rigid insulation is often placed in the airspace.

For economy, especially in newer brick houses, concrete blocks are frequently used for the inner wall, and the interior surface is generally finished with plaster. Interior partitions are usually framed with wood studs, which are covered with wood or wire lath to hold the plaster finish to the walls.

For structural purposes, the tops of door and window openings are covered with lintels made of stone, steel, or cast concrete. Brick arches are a traditional alternative to lintels.

Floor structure

The ends of the floor joists usually rest on recesses in the brick wall. The joists are supported between the perimeter walls with columns or girders. Cross-bracing is nailed between the joists to keep them from twisting. As in wood-framed houses, subflooring is installed over the joists and the finished flooring is applied over the subfloor.

Roof structure

In many brick houses the roof structure is similar to that used in wood-framed houses. But if the roof finish is slate or tile (both of which are extremely heavy), the structure must be reinforced with purlins to support the additional weight.

Foundation problems
Consult an architect or professional engineer when trying to diagnose problems with a foundation.

Settlement
Settlement cracks in walls are not uncommon. If they are not wide and have stabilized, they are not usually a serious problem.

Subsidence
Subsidence is the sinking of a foundation, generally caused by weak or shallow foundations. A wide crack that continues to open is the most common symptom.

Heave
Weak foundations can also be damaged by ground swell or frost heave.

Light foundations
Extensions or bays should never be built on foundations that are lighter or shallower than those supporting the house. If they are, cracks may appear where the two structures meet, as a result of uneven movement between them. This is known as differential movement.

TYPICAL COMPONENTS OF A BRICK HOUSE

1 Tiles or slates	**10** Internal brick wall	**19** Floorboards
2 Ridge board	**11** Brick cavity wall	**20** Ground-floor joists
3 Roof battens	**12** Floor joists	**21** Joist plate
4 Roofing felt	**13** Cross-bracing	**22** Interior support wall
5 Purlin	**14** Plaster ceiling	**23** Damp-proof course
6 Rafters	**15** Brick loadbearing wall	**24** Concrete slab
7 Ceiling joists	**16** Lintel	**25** Concrete footings
8 Wall plate	**17** Block partition	**26** Ground
9 Partition with plaster	**18** Staircase	

Exterior walls

Exterior walls are built to bear the structural loads of the house, to keep out weather and unwanted noises, to trap heat, and to serve as a decorative element in the home's design. There are numerous structural approaches for building exterior walls. The most common ones are illustrated and described below.

Frame wall construction

In wood-framed houses, exterior walls are usually built with 2 x 4 studs nailed 16 inches on center to top and bottom plates. And since exterior walls carry much of the structural load, wall top plates are doubled.

Sheathing is nailed to the outer surface of the wall frame to add rigidity, and is then covered with a weather-resistant membrane. Wood, plywood, hardboard, vinyl, and aluminum sidings are nailed directly to the membrane-covered sheathing. When the exterior finish is made of brick or stucco veneer, there is generally a 1-inch airspace between the sheeting and the veneer.

Fiberglass batt or mineral fiber insulation is frequently used in the stud cavities. A vapor barrier is applied to the interior edges of the wall frame before attaching the interior wall finish, which may be gypsum drywall, plaster, or paneling.

Masonry construction

Very old stone houses may be built with solid walls, but in most masonry construction, cavity walls, consisting of an inner and outer leaf separated by an airspace, are the norm. The two leaves are braced with wall ties running between them, which are then set in the mortar joints. In modern masonry construction, rigid insulation may be set in the airspace, and cement block instead of brick may be used for the inner leaf for economy.

Superinsulated frame walls

In recent years, new approaches to wall framing and insulation have been developed in the interest of conserving energy. Typical of various superinsulation approaches has been the use of 2 x 6 studs and plates to create deeper stud cavities that permit thicker insulation. The added insulation significantly improves the R-value of house walls, a standard that measures structural resistance to the passage of thermal energy.

In addition to improving R-values with thicker insulation and insulated sheathing materials, superinsulating techniques also protect insulation from moisture damage and reduce air infiltration through seams and joints by the application of a vapor barrier. The vapor barrier is carefully wrapped around corners and at floor and ceiling joints. The vapor barrier is also carefully sealed around electrical boxes and other mechanical fixtures.

Semipermeable house wraps have been developed for the membrane between the sheathing and the siding. These permit moisture to escape from the wall cavity but screen out drafts.

Wall ties
Wall ties are laid in the mortar joints and bridge the airspace between the inner and outer leaves of a masonry cavity wall. In brick veneer walls, the ties are fastened to the sheathing.

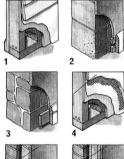

Wire butterfly tie

Sheetmetal tie

Exterior wall construction
1 Frame wall with wood siding
2 Concrete-block wall
3 Solid stone wall
4 Frame wall with stucco veneer
5 Brick cavity wall with block inner leaf
6 Frame wall with brick veneer

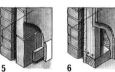

Superinsulated frame wall

When appraising the condition of a house or planning a remodeling project, distinguishing between loadbearing and nonloadbearing walls is critical.

In general, the exterior walls of a house are loadbearing, that is, they transmit the weight of the roof and floor loads of upper stories to the foundation. If you took the finish off exterior walls, you would find that they utilize special structural elements: frame walls have double top plates and thick double headers over window and door openings where the normal stud-spacing pattern is interrupted to bear the weight above. If, when you inspect a house, exterior walls appear to buckle, show unusual cracks, or display vertical or horizontal misalignment, this is evidence of a severe structural problem. If the structural scheme of an exterior wall was altered to build an addition, another way of supporting the loads should have been designed into the job.

Interior walls may be loadbearing or nonloadbearing. If a wall runs parallel to floor joists, chances are it has no structural purpose other than to divide the interior space. But if a wall runs perpendicular to joists and you find a similar wall or columns aligned directly below the wall on a lower story, the wall is loadbearing. A loadbearing wall may also rest on a girder, that is, a heavy horizontal member of steel or wood. Like exterior loadbearing walls, interior bearing walls cannot be removed or structurally altered without providing alternate support. Seek advice from an architect or engineer before proceeding with alterations to loadbearing walls.

Nonloadbearing walls
The orange walls divide the space into smaller rooms, and could be removed without damaging the structure.

Interior walls

The type of interior wall construction and finish will depend to an extent on the building's age and on the wall's function within the structure. Here are the most common types.

Wood-frame walls

Wood framing is by far the most common structural system used for both interior loadbearing and non-loadbearing partitions. Specific structural differences between the two may consist only of a doubled top plate and more extensive cross-bracing in loadbearing walls. In general, wall studs are spaced 16 inches on center and nailed to top and toe plates. In some nonstructural walls, wall studs are spaced 24 inches on center.

In older houses, thin, closely spaced wood lath strips are nailed to the wall frame to serve as a structural basis for plaster. Plaster is usually applied in two coats—an undercoat of brown plaster followed by a finish coat of white plaster. In newer buildings, metal-wire lath is used as the structural base for plaster instead of wood lath. Metal lath over wood studs is also frequently found where the wall finish is ceramic tile set over a mortar base.

In the vast majority of homes built after World War II, interior walls are wood-frame finished with gypsum drywall. The drywall is nailed to the wall frame in sheets, and seams are finished with a drywall joint compound and paper tape. In some cases, a gypsum product similar to drywall is nailed to the wall frame and finished with a skim coat of plaster. Where ceramic tile is applied over a wallboard finish, an adhesive is used as the bonding agent.

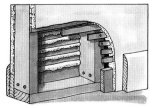

Wood-frame wall with plaster over wood lath

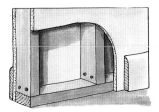

Wood-frame wall with drywall

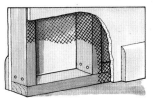

Wood-frame wall with plaster over metal lath

Metal stud walls

In recent years, metal stud systems have begun to be used to construct interior partitions for economy and because of their fire resistance. It is likely that those living in apartment buildings constructed after 1970 will find partitions framed with metal studs and finished with gypsum drywall, which is fastened to the framing with special screws. Metal studs and the track that is used for top and bottom plates are normally U-shaped. These materials are easily cut with tinsnips or aviation shears. Studs are crimped into place in the tracks, which are used for plates, and are easy to remove with a firm twist.

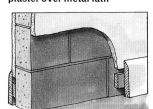

Concrete-block wall finished with plaster

Nonframe walls

In some masonry buildings, especially large apartment buildings constructed between 1890 and 1945, interior partitions may be constructed with lightweight gypsum block or hollow clay block. In most cases with this type of interior wall construction, the wall finish is plaster applied directly to the block. While it is advisable to check with a professional before removing any wall or cutting an opening in it, hollow-block partitions are almost always nonloadbearing. After finding that such a wall serves no critical structural purpose, you can easily break down or open hollow-block walls with a sledgehammer and cold chisel. The top of openings in block walls require a lintel for support.

In modern construction, concrete-block walls are often used as party walls to separate attached housing units. The wall finish may be plaster or gypsum drywall. Concrete-block walls are designed to contain the spread of fires and to provide good sound insulation. Party walls are usually structural and should not be altered without obtaining professional advice and building code permission.

One of the most advanced building technologies—applied increasingly in factory-built, modular homes—is walls made of "stressed-skin panels." While many of the systems are proprietary and the terminology is not entirely uniform, the term usually refers to a wall system that is made with an inner core of rigid foam insulation to which plywood, particleboard, or drywall has been laminated. The panels have interlocking joints. Never alter a stressed-skin panel structure without consulting the manufacturer.

Glass blocks
Hollow glass blocks can be used for nonloadbearing walls. Made in square and rectangular shapes and a range of colors, they are usually laid in mortar.

Converting two rooms to one

Removing a wall may be the best way to improve access between areas frequently used, the dining and living rooms, for instance, and to expand your living space in other areas of the house. Removing a dividing wall, whether it's structural or simply a nonloadbearing partition, is a major undertaking. But it doesn't have to be overwhelming. If you follow some basic safety and structural rules, much of the job is straightforward, albeit very messy and disruptive. Before you start, plan out your requirements and consult the flow chart, right, for a breakdown of just what's involved.

● **Hiring professionals**
If you're in doubt, hire a professional builder. To save costs, you may be able to work as a laborer or do preparation and clearing work.

Why do you want to remove a wall?

Before you go ahead and demolish the wall between two rooms, consider just how the new space might function, its appearance, the time it will take you to carry out the work, and the cost.

Ask yourself the following questions: Will the shape and size of the new room suit your needs? Remember, if you have a young family, your needs are likely to change as they grow up.

Will most of the family activities be carried out in the same room (eating, watching television, playing music, reading, conversation, playing with toys, hobbies, homework)?

Will removing the wall deprive you of privacy within the family, or from passersby in the street?

Will the new room feel like one unit and not a conversion? For example, do the baseboards and moldings match?

Should one of the doorways, if close to another, be blocked off?

Will the loss of a wall make the furniture arrangements difficult, particularly if radiators are in use and take up valuable wall space elsewhere?

Will the heating and lighting need to be modified?

Will the proposed shape of the opening be in character with the room and in the right proportion?

Removing a wall: Planning ahead

Procedure for removing a loadbearing or nonloadbearing wall. Follow red for loadbearing, blue for nonloadbearing.

PLANNING
Consider function, appearance, time, and cost.

Assess if the wall is loadbearing or nonloadbearing.

NONLOADBEARING

LOADBEARING
Submit plan to building department.

Obtain approval.

PROCEED

Mark out opening.

● **Planning advice**
If you are in any doubt about calculating the correct size of beam, consult a structural engineer and/or the building inspector.

Calculate beam size. Select and buy materials.

Rent steel props and scaffold boards.

PREPARE THE WALL
Remove baseboard. Hang dust sheets.

Cut off electricity to switches and receptacles, then reroute the wiring.

REMOVE PARTITION WALL

Remove drywall or lath-and-plaster surface.

FIT BEAM
Set up temporary structural support.

Position props and temporary plates.

● **Rubbish disposal**
Don't forget to order a dumpster or organize some method of getting rid of the debris. Salvage bricks and lumber for future use.

Remove wall finish.

Install vertical supports for beam.

If it's a nonloadbearing block wall, remove individual blocks from the top.

Remove blocking and studs.

Lift beam onto support columns and level it.

Remove top and bottom plates.

FINISH OFF
Finish beam and walls as required.

FINISH FLOOR
Close up the floor gaps or level the floors between rooms.

Finish ceiling and wall gaps.

Removing a loadbearing wall

I f a loadbearing wall is to be removed to create a more open plan, a beam must be installed to maintain the home's structural integrity. The basic options for removing a loadbearing wall are discussed below.

Structural concerns

An interior loadbearing wall generally supports the weight of an upper floor and sometimes, depending on the design, part of the weight of the roof. When a loadbearing wall is removed, provisions must be made to support the loads on that wall. Typically, a horizontal beam is installed in the area where joists of the upper floor rested on the top plate of the wall that is being removed. The beam is supported by vertical columns that transmit the load to the foundation and other structural elements of the house frame.

The size of the beam is determined by several factors: the load it must bear, the span between the vertical columns that support it, the distance from the beam to other structural elements that run parallel to it, the material from which the beam is made, and local standards for minimum floor-load capacities. While determining the necessary size required for a beam in any given situation is a matter for a professional engineer, architect, or building official, in general, the greater the load, span between vertical supports, and distance from parallel structural elements, the larger the beam must be. The required thickness and depth of a beam can be changed, based on the number and spacing of support columns and with the introduction of other structural elements running parallel to the beam.

Choosing a beam

Beams of several different materials can be used to provide structural support where a loadbearing wall is removed. In many cases, rolled steel I-beams are used. Because of steel's great strength, the depth of the beam can be relatively shallow compared with the other options. And this can be an important concern where maximum headroom for an opening is critical. But steel beams can present some difficulties for typical do-it-yourselfers. Most codes require that steel beams be supported by steel columns, and that connections be either welded or bolted—both options that require special equipment and skills. Finishing a steel beam can also be difficult.

Laminated wood beams are a desirable option preferred by do-it-yourselfers and increasingly specified by architects. The beams are made by laminating multiple pieces of lumber. Several appearance grades are available which may either be finished with drywall or left exposed for decorative effect. Laminated beams can be cut and drilled with ordinary tools, and can be joined to columns with structural joints, lagscrews, or approved metal fastening plates.

Planning and approval

In most areas, it is necessary to obtain a building permit before removing a load-bearing wall. To obtain a permit, you have to provide the inspector with drawings that include key details of the existing structure and specs for the installation of new support components. While a knowledgeable do-it-yourselfer may be able to prepare such drawings, others should hire an architect or structural engineer.

Once your plans are approved—and you've paid a fee—work can begin. The inspector will stipulate a schedule for various inspections and it's your responsibility to tell the inspector when the various stages are complete.

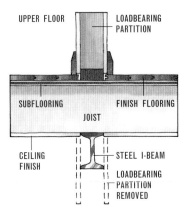

Steel I-beam bears load where structural wall is removed

How a beam is supported

Beams are supported by vertical columns that transmit the load to other structural elements within the building. The required number and spacing of columns is contingent on the load and the size of the beam.

The drawing below illustrates a typical situation. The structural beam supporting the second-floor joists is supported by a column that transmits the weight to the end of a girder notched into the foundation wall. As you move to the left, you see another column supporting the beam. That column bears directly on the girder and aligns with a column supporting it.

The key point is that columns must align either exactly or very nearly to maintain the structural integrity of the beam. Note that a concrete footing appears below the basement floor slab beneath the columns to bear and spread the weight of the imposed load.

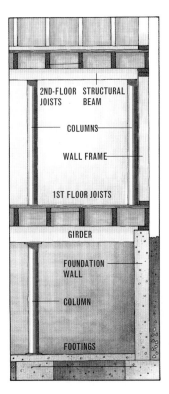

Opening masonry walls

Safe propping procedure

To remove part of a masonry wall you must temporarily support the wall above the opening. You will need to rent adjustable steel jacks and scaffold boards on which to support them.

Where the beam is to be placed at ceiling level, rent extra boards to support the ceiling **(1)**. Generally you will have to install short beams through the wall to transfer the load to the jacks **(2)**. These beams must measure at least 4 x 6 inches.

Rent sufficient jacks to be spaced not more than 3 feet apart across the width of the opening. If possible, buy the beam after the initial inspection by the building inspector. It can then be cut to your exact requirements.

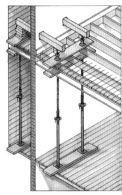

1 Layout for removing wall flush with ceiling

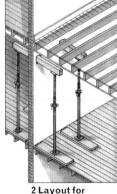

2 Layout for removing wall below ceiling

Preparation

Remove the baseboards from both sides of the wall. Working from one side, mark out the position of the beam on the wall in pencil. Use a steel tape measure, level, and straightedge for accuracy. Hang dust sheets or drop cloths around the work area on the opposite face of the wall to help contain the airborne dust. Seal gaps around all doors with masking tape to prevent the dust from traveling throughout the house. Open windows in the rooms you're working in.

Inserting support beams

Mark the position for the support beams on the wall, then cut away the plaster and chisel a hole through the brickwork at each point. Finish the hole at the bottom of one course of bricks. Make the holes slightly oversize so you can easily pass the beams through. Position a pair of adjustable jacks under each beam not more than 2 feet from each side of the wall. Stand the jacks on scaffold boards to spread the load over the floor.

Adjust the jacks to take the weight of the structure and nail their baseplates to the supporting boards to prevent them from being dislodged.

Supporting the ceiling

If the ceiling needs supporting, stand the jacks on scaffold boards at each side of the wall and adjust them so they're just below ceiling height. (They should be placed 2 feet from the wall.) Place another plank on top of the jacks and adjust the jacks until the ceiling joists are supported.

Removing the wall

Brick-cutting saw

Chip off plaster with a sledge-hammer and cold chisel, then cut out the brickwork, working from the top. Once you've removed four or five courses, cut the bricks on the side of the opening. Chisel down pointing to cut the bricks cleanly. Remove all brickwork down to one course below the floorboards. Clear the rubble into garbage bags as you work. If you are removing a lot of debris, it may be worth renting a dumpster. The job is slow and laborious, but a circular saw with a masonry blade can make it easier and quicker.

To reduce the risk of structural collapse when opening up walls, it is critical to set up jacks in a safe manner. Use a level to make sure that jacks are plumb and always use heavy boards running perpendicular to the floor joists at the jack bearing points to spread the load. If the floor structure on which jacks are bearing seems springy, set jack posts directly beneath them on the floor below.

Jacks passing through suspended floor

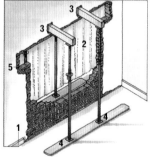

Cutting the opening

1 Remove or cut back the baseboard and mark the beam's position.
2 Hang dust sheets around the work area.
3 Cut openings and insert support beams.
4 Stand jacks on scaffold boards and adjust them to support the beams.
5 Cut away the plaster, then chisel out the bricks starting from the top of the opening.

Lightweight partition walls that are not loadbearing can be removed safely without consulting the authorities for approval and without the need to add temporary supports. You must, however, be certain that the wall is not structural before doing so because some partitions do offer partial structural support.

Dismantling a stud partition

Remove the baseboards from both sides of the wall and any other moldings. It's a good idea to save these for reuse or repairs in the future. If any electrical switches, receptacles, or light fixtures are attached to the wall, they must be disconnected and rerouted before work begins.

Removing the plasterwork

Use a claw hammer or crowbar to remove the drywall or plaster and lath covering the wall frame. Be sure to wear gloves, goggles, long pants and shirt, and a respirator when doing this work. Remove the debris for disposal.

Removing the framework

First knock away any blocking from between the studs. Then pull out the studs. If they are difficult to remove, saw through them at an angle, to prevent the saw from binding. If you make the cut close to the top or bottom plate, you will be left with useful lumber for future work.

Pry the top and bottom plates from the ceiling joists and floor. If the end studs are nailed to the walls, pry them away with a crowbar.

Finishing off

Fill any gaps in the ceiling and walls by installing narrow strips of drywall. If you have a gap in your flooring, fill it with stock that's the same size and kind of wood.

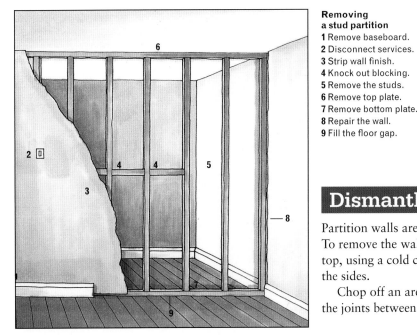

Removing a stud partition
1 Remove baseboard.
2 Disconnect services.
3 Strip wall finish.
4 Knock out blocking.
5 Remove the studs.
6 Remove top plate.
7 Remove bottom plate.
8 Repair the wall.
9 Fill the floor gap.

Closing a floor gap

When you remove a wall to create one room from two or part of a wall to create a passage, a gap may be left in the finish flooring where the bottom plate of the wall had been fastened to the subflooring.

If a gap runs parallel to the direction of the boards in wood-strip flooring, you can fill it with little disturbance to the pattern. Since floorboards are generally milled with a tongue on one edge and a groove on the other so that they interlock when they are installed, fitting new boards into a confined space can present a problem. If the protruding tongue of an existing floorboard will not allow you to set the filler board in place, chisel away the lower edge of the groove so the filler board can drop over the tongue. If the filler board must be ripped to a narrower width, cut a rabbet to fit over the tongue.

If the gap runs perpendicular to the existing flooring, it will look better to fill it with strips running in the same direction rather than with short strips to match the existing pattern. In this case, match the groove side of a filler board against the ends of existing flooring at one side of the gap and drive finish nails through the tongue. This technique is called blind nailing. Fit the grooves of subsequent rows over the tongues of installed strips and nail in the same way. To fit the final strip in place, remove the tongue with a saw or hand plane, then push the board in place. The last board will need to be face nailed.

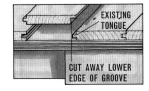

Gap parallel to floorboards — EXISTING TONGUE, CUT AWAY LOWER EDGE OF GROOVE

Gap perpendicular to floorboards — BLIND NAIL, FACE NAIL, REMOVE TONGUE

Dismantling a block wall

Partition walls are sometimes made using lightweight concrete blocks. To remove the wall, start to cut away the individual units from the top, using a cold chisel and hammer. Work from the center out toward the sides.

Chop off an area of plaster or drywall first, so that you can locate the joints between individual blocks.

Aligning mismatched floors

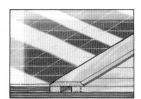

Installing a saddle
Install filler blocks in gap and nail saddle to blocks.

Installing a molding strip
Install quarter-round molding to finish and protect tile edge.

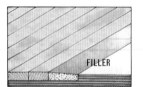

Filling with cementitious filler
Slope the patch from one level to the other. Finish with carpet or vinyl flooring.

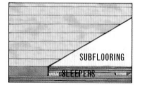

Building up lower floor surface
Match the higher surface with sleepers and subflooring. Treat subflooring or both surfaces.

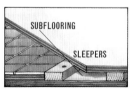

Setting sleepers
Use sleepers to equalize the height on the lower surface, and set subflooring over both surfaces.

When a partition wall separating two rooms is removed or when an opening is made to create a passageway, sometimes the levels of the finished flooring on the two sides of the wall are at different heights. This usually happens when the finished flooring of one room is different from the other, or when a floor has been refinished during a previous remodeling project. For the sake of both appearance and safety, you must provide an appropriate transition between the two levels. Several possible solutions to the problem are discussed below.

Treating slight mismatches

The slightest mismatch in floor levels can cause people to trip. When a slight mismatch exists, it is desirable to create a distinct visual transition between the two floor surfaces that will catch people's attention. Then they will walk more carefully.

For example, a slight mismatch could exist when one part of a floor surface is finished with ceramic tile and the remainder with wood-strip flooring. Ordinarily, the tile floor could be anywhere from ¼ to ⅞ inch higher than the wood floor, due to the extra subflooring that is usually installed beneath tile. There are three simple ways to correct this problem.

The first is to install a saddle to cover the gap left by the wall that has been removed. The best way to do this is to fill the gap with wood blocks or strips level with the wood floor. The saddle, a stock molding available in several widths at any lumberyard, is then nailed in place over the filler blocks. The top of the saddle should be level with or slightly higher than the higher of the two surfaces. In most cases saddles are finished with a stain to match the adjacent floors and then covered with at least three coats of polyurethane varnish. They can also be painted, but be sure to use a high-quality enamel paint. Prime the saddle and paint on at least two topcoats.

A second alternative is to nail a small quarter-round molding to the edge of the tile subflooring. This provides the appropriate visual transition and also protects the tile edge from cracking.

A third solution that would unify the room and address a slight mismatch in floor levels would be to fill the gap with a cementitious floor-filling compound finished with a slope to make the transition from one level to the other. The method is used when the entire floor surface is going to be covered with carpeting.

Building up floor levels

When you want to create a uniform floor level in two rooms that have been made into one by removing a partition, you can build up the existing floor to create a flat, uniform plane. The methods and materials you choose are based on the amount of differential between the existing floors. This involves installing new subflooring on one or both sides of the gap and, in extreme cases, can also require installing sleepers on the lower floor to support the new subflooring.

Before you make a decision on one of the specific approaches illustrated on this page, it is important to consider what type and thicknesses of materials constitute adequate subflooring for various floor finishes. Plywood, particleboard, tempered hardboard, and fiberboard are generally used for subflooring. Pine, plywood, and hardboard strips can be used for sleepers.

Ceramic and vinyl tile and laminated wood flooring boards require a fairly rigid subfloor to prevent them from flexing underfoot, which would ultimately loosen the adhesive and might result in cracking. For these applications, a minimum thickness of ½-inch plywood or ⅝-inch particleboard is recommended. If these materials are to be supported by sleepers, the spacing between the sleepers should be no greater than 16 inches. Tempered hardboard can be used as subflooring for tiles only if it is laid directly over an existing floor without sleepers.

Solid wood-strip flooring, which is generally 1 inch thick, can be nailed directly to an existing wood floor, to any existing sturdy subfloor, or perpendicular to sleepers spaced 16 inches apart. Sleepers and subflooring should be fastened either with screws or with ring-shank nails that resist popping. Fasteners should be approximately three times longer than the thickness of the material being fastened. Adhesive can be used along with fasteners.

While constructing stud walls finished with gypsum drywall is a simple, convenient way to attain visual privacy, the conventional system of framing and finishing provides low resistance to sound transmission. The typical wall, framed with 2 x 4s and finished with ½-inch drywall, has a sound transmission rating (STC) of only 30 to 34.

Filling stud cavities with batt insulation and using thicker drywall, even doubling the layers of drywall, will improve the resistance to sound transmission. One of the most effective approaches to the problem, however, is to modify the wall framing by using lumber for the top and bottom plates that is wider than that used for the studs. Studs are then fastened in place on 8-inch centers, with edges alternately aligned with opposite edges of the plates.

This reduces the amount of sound-induced vibration that is transmitted from one side of the wall to the other. The STC rating of the model illustrated below, which uses 2 x 4 studs set on 2 x 6 plates and is finished with double layers of ⅝-inch drywall, would have a rating of 50 to 54—nearly equal to that of a 7-inch-thick brick cavity wall.

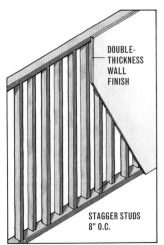

DOUBLE-THICKNESS WALL FINISH

STAGGER STUDS 8" O.C.

Wall framing and finishing designed to reduce sound transmission

Constructing partitions to divide larger spaces into smaller ones or to alter an existing floor plan is, for the most part, a relatively simple matter. You just construct one or more stud walls and finish the surfaces with drywall or another wall finish. Considerations relating to codes, design goals, and methods of construction are discussed here and on the following pages.

Code considerations

Code regulations concerning the construction of partition walls vary widely from locale to locale. But in general, they govern the amount and type of ventilation that must be provided within an enclosed space, minimum dimensions for hallways, and fire safety provisions. For example, most rooms that can be categorized as living space (living rooms, dining areas, bedrooms, and the like), must have windows of a certain size in relation to the square footage of the room in order to provide adequate light and ventilation. Bathrooms and kitchens, while not necessarily required to have windows, frequently are required to have mechanical ventilation.

With respect to fire regulations, the type and thickness of materials used to construct partitions are frequently specified to ensure that walls can withstand or contain fire for a minimum of 1 hour. For multiple dwellings in some urban areas, metal studs are required and wood studs are not permitted.

Many local codes specify that hallways may be no less than 3 feet wide to provide sufficient room for passage. While it is a good idea to consult with your local building department for code standards relating to your particular project, it's also important to think through the space requirements for activities and room furnishings so that you will arrive at a workable, comfortable design.

Positioning a partition

The frame for a partition wall is generally made from 2 x 4 lumber and consists of a top plate, which is attached to the ceiling, a bottom plate, which is attached to the floor, and studs, which run vertically between the two plates. It is not usually necessary to remove the existing ceiling, floor, or wall finish to fasten a new wall frame to existing structural elements. But you do have to make sure that the fasteners you use are driven into existing structural members. As a rule of thumb, use fasteners that are two to three times as long as the plate is thick.

Determine first whether the new partition will run perpendicular or parallel to existing floor and ceiling joists. If it will run perpendicular, be sure to establish the exact location of the joists. (Floor joists are usually spaced on 16-inch centers, ceiling joists on 16- or 24-inch centers.) Drive the fasteners through the plates and into the joists.

If the partition is to run parallel with joists, center the plates on a joist or add blocking between existing joists to provide structural anchoring for fasteners. An end stud that abuts an existing wall should be nailed or screwed to a stud in the existing wall. If a stud does not fall where the new wall ends, either open up the wall and add some blocking or use toggle bolts to hold the new wall in place. Use expansion bolts to anchor to masonry walls.

Right-angle alignment
A partition set at right angles to joists is well supported.

Parallel alignment
A partition parallel with the joists must be supported by one of them.

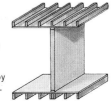

Building a stud partition

1 Snap chalkline on ceiling

2 Mark top and bottom plate together

3 Mark door opening on top plate first

4 Prop top plate against ceiling

5 Nail header between studs

Making a stud partition wall is the easiest way to divide a room in two. You can construct a plain wall, or add a doorway, pass-through, or glazed area to "borrow" light from an existing window.
You can build the partition directly onto the floorboards or the joists below. The ends of the partition can be set against the existing wall finish provided there is a stud or other solid material directly under it, or the existing wall can be opened to add the necessary structural member.

Using a chalkline
A retractable self-coating chalkline makes layout easier.

Laying out and spacing the studs

Mark the position of one edge of the bottom plate for the new wall on the floor in chalk. Use a chalkline or a length of 2 x 4 as a guide to draw the line. Continue the guidelines up the walls at each side, using a level and a straight board. Continue the guidelines onto the ceiling, by snapping a chalkline onto the surface (1).

Spacing the studs
Lay the top and bottom plates together with their face sides facing upward. Mark the position of the studs at 16-inch centers working from one edge. Square the lines across both members with a square (2). Center a 2 x 4 scrap over the layout marks and use the edges as a guide for marking the stud positions. If you are installing ⅜-inch drywall or solid tongue-and-groove paneling, 24-inch spacing can be used.

Laying out a doorway
If you are including a doorway in the wall, make allowance for the width of the opening. The studs that form the sides of the opening must be spaced apart by the width of the door plus the thickness of both doorjambs, plus ½ inch of adjustment space on both sides. Mark the width of the opening on the top plate at the required positions, then transfer these marks to the bottom plate and cut out the opening in the bottom plate (3). The door studs overlap the ends of the bottom plates, which must be cut back to allow for them.

Attaching the framework

Secure the bottom plate to the floor on each side of the door opening using 16d nails or 4-inch lagscrews. Use the top plate as a guide to keep the two bottom-plate boards in line.
Brace the top plate against the ceiling on its line and check that the stud marks on the top plate line up with those on the bottom plate (4). Use a straight board and a level or a plumb bob to do this. Nail or screw the top plate through the ceiling finish and into the joists above.
Measure the distance between the top and bottom plate at each end and cut the outer wall studs to length. They should fit tightly between the plates. Fasten the end studs to the walls with nails or screws.

Attaching door studs
Cut the door studs to fit between the plates and wedge them in place but do not fasten them yet. Mark the position of the door header on the studs. Allow for the door height, the jamb thickness, and ⅛ inch of adjustment room.

Attaching the rough header
Nail the door studs to the plates, then nail the header in place through the studs (5). Install short studs, called cripple studs, above the header.

Alternative fastening for door studs

Double door studs
1 Jack studs
2 Full studs
3 Header

Another method for framing a door opening is to double up the studs on both sides. On the outside are two full studs, but next to them are nailed shorter studs, called jack studs. The jack studs align with the door opening and provide direct support for the header.

Once the header is nailed in place, cut short lengths of 2 x 4 to fit vertically between the top plate and the header. These cripple studs provide nailing surfaces for the wall finish that's installed later. Make sure when nailing all the parts together that their faces are flush, the studs are plumb, and the header is level. The size of the rough opening must be large enough to accommodate the new door with all the necessary clearances.

Stud partitions

Fastening studs and blocking

Measure and cut each full-length stud and fasten these to the plates (see below). Cut the blocking to fit between the studs and, working from the wall, toenail the first end to the wall stud, then nail through the next stud into the end of the block. One or two rows of blocking may be required. To install drywall horizontally, place the center

Space studs equally and nail top and bottom

Nail blocking between studs to stiffen them

of the blocks 4 feet below the ceiling. To install drywall vertically, install the blocking in the middle of the wall, staggering it to facilitate blocking.

Fastening to an existing stud wall

Partitions are used for interior walls of rooms. If your new partition meets a wood-frame wall, align it with the framing members in the existing wall.

Fasten the end stud of the new partition to a stud in the existing wall. Locate the stud by drilling closely spaced holes through the wall finish to find the center of the stud.

When the new partition wall falls between the studs of the existing wall, nail the end stud to the blocking and the plates of the existing wall. If you can't get solid nailing, you can use toggle bolts to hold the end stud to the existing wall. Or you can open up the old wall, install a new stud in it, then replace the old wall finish. This is the most difficult option, but it may be the only way to get good support.

Fastening drywall vertically

Start at the doorway with the edge of the first sheet flush with the stud face. Before fastening, cut a 1-inch-wide strip on both sides of the sheet where it falls over the header space.

Fasten the board with 1¼- or 1½-inch nails not more than 12 inches apart. Install the sheets on both sides of the doorway, then cut and install a piece to cover the header space. Allow a ⅛-inch gap at the butt joint. Install the remaining boards.

Fastening drywall horizontally

Drywall can be installed horizontally where it is more economical or convenient to do so. Nail the top row of sheets in place first, followed by the bottom row. If the sheets in the bottom row have to be cut to height, remember to install the cut edge down so it falls behind the baseboard.

Temporarily nail a horizontal support board to the studs ⅛-inch below the centerline of the blocking. Lift a sheet onto the strip, adjust it from side to side until the ends of the sheet fall over the middle of the studs, and nail the sheet in place. Install the remainder of the top sheets in this way. Then install the bottom row. Make sure to stagger the joints between sheets so they don't line up with the joints in the top row.

You'll need help from a second person to carry the sheets and to hold them while you are nailing. Always nail from the center of the sheet to the outside edges. This keeps the sheet flat against the studs.

Use two 10d common nails to toenail each butt joint, one through each side. When driving in the first nail, temporarily nail a block behind the stud to prevent it from moving sideways, or hold your foot against the back side of the stud. Blocks cut to fit between each stud can be permanently nailed in place to provide extra support.

Alternative stud-nailing method

For a very rigid frame, set the studs into ½-inch-deep dadoes notched into the top and bottom plates.

Toenailing
Toenail a butt joint with two nails.

Nailing technique
Support the stud with a block while driving the first nail.

Supporting joint
Blocks nailed to each side brace the joint.

Dado joints
Dado joints make for a very rigid frame.

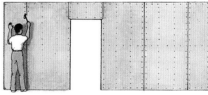

Installing drywall vertically
Work away from doorway or start at one end.

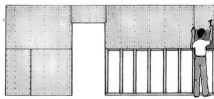

Installing drywall horizontally
Install top row first, then stagger joints on bottom row.

Building a staggered partition

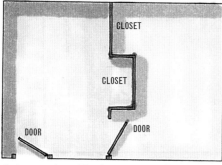

A staggered partition forms storage closets on each side, one for each room.

A stud wall can be built to divide one room into two and provide closet space at the same time. The construction is the same as described for the straight partition, except for the right-angle junctions.

Constructing a staggered partition with a door at one end and a spacious closet in the middle, as shown below, makes sensible use of available space.

Positioning the wall

Mark out the bottom-plate position of the main partition across the floor. Mark the position of the recessed partition parallel with it. For clothes storage the recess should be at least 2 feet deep.

Calculate the length of the wall segments by laying them out on the floor. Starting from the wall adjacent to the doorway, measure off the thickness of a stud, the doorjamb, the width of the door, and the finished jamb. Also add ½ inch for clearance around the door. This takes you to the closet opening. Measure from this point to the other existing wall and divide the dimension in two. This gives you the other side of the closet opening. Lay out the remainder of the walls on the floor.

Fastening the top and bottom plates

Mark the position for the top plates on the ceiling. Use a straightedge and a level or plumb bob to ensure that the stud marks on both plates line up exactly. Cut and nail the bottom and top plates to the floor and ceiling, as described earlier for a straight stud partition. Cut and install the studs at the required spacing to suit the thickness of the wall finish. Cut and nail headers and blocking in place.

The right-angled corners and the end of the short partition, which supports the doorframe, need extra studs to stiffen the wall and to provide a nailing surface for the drywall.

Make up a corner from three studs as shown below. Install short 2 x 4 blocks between the studs as spacers **(1)**. For the end of the partition next to the doorway, join two studs with blocks **(2)**. Always nail these blocks flush with the edges of the studs they join.

Once all the wall sections are built and nailed together, check for square and plumb. Then hang drywall on both sides of all the walls. Overlap the corners of the drywall sheets **(3)**. At the door opening leave half of the last stud exposed to provide nailing for the drywall that covers the door framing. Assemble the doorframe, including both studs, header, cripple studs, and top plate, then lift it into place. Attach one door stud to the partition and cover it with drywall **(4)**. Attach the other door stud to the wall **(5)** and finish trimming out the door.

Building the wall

1 Mark the bottom-plate stud positions.
2 Transfer the marks to the top plates.
3 Cut and fasten the bottom plates to the floor.
4 Nail the top plates to the ceiling.
5 Make corners from three studs.
6 Nail the other studs at required spacing.
7 Add blocking.
8 Install doorframe.

1 Corner
Use three studs at the partition corners.

2 End post
Use two studs at the end of the partition.

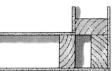

3 Overlap drywall at corners

4 Attach one door stud to partition.

5 Attach other stud to wall.

Fastening to a stud wall

Unlike solid brick or block walls, stud walls are mainly hollow, presenting problems when you need to hang wall fixtures. Ideally fixtures should be fastened directly to structural framing members for maximum support. But if fixture positions can't be changed, extra studs, or blocking, should be incorporated into the wall before the wall finish is installed.

Mounting a basin

A wall-mounted basin will need sound enough support to carry its own weight and that of someone leaning on it when it's being used.

Buy the basin before building the wall, or work from the manufacturer's literature, which usually specifies the distance between centers for attaching the brackets. Position two studs to take the mounting screws. Mark the center lines of the studs on the floor before applying the drywall or plaster, then draw plumb lines from the marks up onto the wall surface. Measure the height from the floor for the brackets and fasten them securely with screws.

Another approach would be to install a plywood mounting board to fit between the studs to carry both the

basin and the faucets, if they are not mounted on the basin. Use exterior-grade plywood at least ¾ inch thick.

Screw 2 x 2 nailing strips to the inside faces of the studs, set back from the front edges by the thickness of the plywood. Cut the panel to size, then nail it to the nailers so it's flush with the edges of the studs.

Install the wall finish to the side of the wall that will carry the basin, leaving the other side open for water supply pipes and drain lines. Drill holes in the plates for pipes. If any pipes need to run sideways, across the wall, notch the studs as shown on the far right. Fasten the basin support brackets through the wall covering and into the plywood block, using lagbolts.

Cabinets and shelves

It is not always possible to arrange studs as needed for mounting things on the wall. If there are no studs where you want them, you will have to use hollow-wall fasteners instead. Choose a type that will adequately support the cabinet.

One good choice is toggle bolts (see right). These pieces of hardware are pushed through holes drilled in the back of the cabinet and the wall. The spring-loaded wings on the end of the bolt expand when they get through the hole. A washer keeps the screwhead against the cabinet back. By tightening the screw, you pull the bolt wings against the inside surface of the wallcovering. Once the bolt is tight, the back of the cabinet and the wallcovering are sandwiched securely together. For most cabinets, install a toggle bolt at each corner of the back panel.

Wall-mounted bookshelves have to carry a considerable weight, so be sure to pick heavy-duty hardware for the job. Use a shelving system that has strong metal uprights that hold and support adjustable brackets. Screw the uprights into studs for the most secure support.

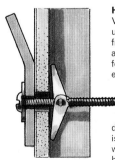

Hollow-wall fasteners
Various fasteners can be used for hanging items from a wall where studs are not available. Some feature screws housed in expanding sheaths. The sheaths expand and press against the sides of the hole when the screw is driven in. Another option is a toggle bolt that has wings that spring out behind the wallcovering as the screw is tightened.

Toggle bolt

It is easy to plan and install pipes and electrical cables in a stud partition wall before finishing it. To guard against future occupants drilling into them, install horizontal runs of pipe and cable no more than 12 inches above the floor.

Plumbing

Plan the runs of supply or waste pipes by marking the faces of the studs, plates, and blocking. Remember that a waste pipe must have a slight fall toward the main waste pipe. When the layout is set, cut notches in the studs for the pipes.

Transfer the marked lines to the sides of the studs or blocking and drill holes for the pipes in the middle of these framing members. Cut in to the holes to make notches for the pipe.

Also make ¾-inch-deep notches in the outside edge of the studs to receive 1 x 2 fillers that bridge the notch to reinforce the studs. Install the pipes, followed by the fillers. Make sure the fillers are flush with the edges of the studs. You don't have to add filler strips to any notches that you cut in the blocking.

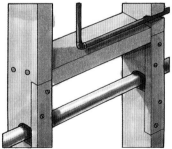

Running plumbing through a stud wall
Reinforce studs with filler pieces.

Running electric cable

Drill ⅝-inch holes at the centers of the studs and blocking for running electrical cable. When framing members are exposed, mount electrical boxes against the studs or blocking for rigid support. Boxes are available with different types of brackets for this purpose. But if you need to install a box after the

Attach electrical boxes to framing member

wallcovering is in place, use cut-in boxes designed to mount directly into holes cut in the drywall or plaster surface.

Suspended ceiling systems

A high ceiling can be a practical liability. It increases heating bills and makes ceiling repairs more difficult. Lowering the ceiling can help solve these problems and cover up a problem ceiling at the same time. Suspended ceiling systems are made from lightweight metal tracks that hold acoustic or translucent panels. They are easy to install, and don't require specialized tools.

The basic system

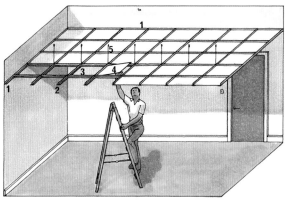

Lightweight suspended ceiling
1 Wall angle
2 Main runner
3 Cross runner
4 Ceiling panels
5 Wire hangers

The lightweight alloy framework is made from three basic elements: wall angles, which are fastened to walls; main runners, which are similar in function to joists and are usually installed across a room's shorter span; and cross runners, which are set between and perpendicular to main runners. The loose panels sit on the flanges of the runners. They can be easily lifted out for access to ducts or to service light fixtures, which can be concealed behind them. You need at least 4 inches of space above the framework to install the panels.

Setting out the grid

Normally, 2 x 2-foot or 2 x 4-foot panels are used for suspended ceiling systems. Before installing the framework, draw a plan of the ceiling on graph paper to ensure that the borders are symmetrical. Draw two lines at the halfway point of each wall that bisect in the middle. Lay out the grid on your plan with a main runner centered on the short bisecting line **(1)**. Then lay it out again with a line of panels centered on the same line **(2)**. Use the grid that provides the widest border panels. Plot the position of the cross runners in the same way, using the other line **(3, 4)**. Try to get the border panels even on opposite sides of the room **(5)**.

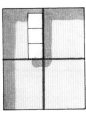

1 Main runner on center

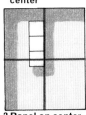

2 Panel on center

3 Center cross runner

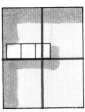

4 Panel on center

5 Best grid arrangement

Installing the framework

Before installing a suspended ceiling that has translucent panels under fluorescent light fixtures, remove any flaking material and repair any cracks in the ceiling above. Paint the ceiling with white latex paint to reflect more light from the fixtures.

Install fluorescent light fixtures as needed across the ceiling (16 watts per square yard is recommended as a suitable level of light in most rooms).

Mark the height of the suspended ceiling on the walls with a continuous level line around the whole room. Using a hacksaw or tinsnips, cut lengths of wall angle to fit the longest walls. Mark the stud locations on the wall, then hold up the wall angles and transfer these marks to the angles. Drill screw holes through the angles and attach them to the walls with screws **(1)**. Next, cut lengths of wall angle to fit the shorter walls. Their ends should fit on the angles already installed.

Mark the positions of the runners, using your graph-paper plan as a guide. Cut the main runners to span the room. Place their ends on the wall angles **(2)**. Use a ceiling panel to check that they are parallel and at right angles to the wall and each other.

Install full-sized cross runners between the main runners according to your plan. Then, cut the border cross runners to fit between the main runners and the wall angles. Align them with the layout marks on the wall. Install the other cross runners in the same way.

Working from the center, drop in the full-sized panels. Measure and cut the border panels to fit the grid and then drop them into place.

1 Screw angle to wall

2 Position main runners

Installing a folding ladder

Attic access hatches

Access to the attic space is more convenient and safer if you install a folding ladder. Some come complete with built-in hatch cover, frame, and hardware ready to install in a new opening. Normally, the length of the ladders suits standard ceiling heights, between 7 feet 6 inches and 8 feet. Some extend up to 10 feet.

To install an accordion ladder, securely screw the brackets of the aluminum ladder to the framework of the opening. Install the retaining hooks to the framework to support the ladder in the stowed position. Operate the ladder with a pole, which hooks over the bottom rail. Install the hatch door to the frame with a continuous hinge, followed by the latch that's installed on the other end of the hatch door.

Accordion ladder

For a ready-to-install folding ladder, cut the opening and trim the joists to the size specified by the maker. Insert the unit in the opening and screw it to the joists.

Many houses are provided with a hatch in the ceiling to give access to the attic space for convenient storage and maintenance of the roof structure. If your house has a large attic space without access from inside the house, installing a hatch could be a valuable addition. Hatch units are available at many home centers. Although the job is straightforward, it does require cutting into the ceiling structure.

When cutting into the structure of a ceiling to create an attic entrance, it's important to consider the effect of the alteration on the ability of the framing to support the existing structure. Some roof frames may incorporate purlins, which are sometimes supported by vertical members that transfer part of the roof load to ceiling joists. If you have any doubts about the effect of cutting joists to install a hatch, consult an architect or engineer.

If you have a choice, site the hatch over a hallway, but not close to the stairs. Access is usually easy from a hallway without having to move furniture, which is more likely if you install it in a bedroom. Make sure your location will provide enough attic headroom so you can climb through the hatch.

Making the opening

If you are planning to install a special folding ladder, the size of the new opening will be specified by the manufacturer. Aim to cut away no more than one of the ceiling joists, usually spaced 16 inches apart.

Locate three of the joists by drilling pilot holes in the ceiling. Mark out a square for the opening between the two outer joists. Cut an inspection hole inside the marked area to check that no obstacles are in the way of the cutlines. Saw through the ceiling material and strip it away.

Hold a light into the roof space and climb up between the joists. Lay a board across the joists to support yourself. Saw through the middle joist, cutting it back 3 inches from each edge of the opening. Cut four new pieces of joist lumber to fit between the uncut joists. Use two of these pieces for a header at each end of the cut joist. Nail the headers between the joists using 16d common nails.

Nail the ceiling lath or drywall to the underside of the header joists. Cut jambs from ¾-inch-thick boards to cover the joists and the edges of the ceiling finish. Repair any damage to the ceiling around the opening.

Cut and nail casing boards around the opening to finish it off. If you plan to use a hinged door, install the casing boards flush to the opening. If you want a simple drop-in panel instead, install the casing boards so they overlap the hatch opening by ¾ inch on all sides. Then cut the panel, push it through the opening, and let it rest on the edges of the casing boards.

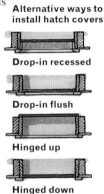

Alternative ways to install hatch covers

Drop-in recessed

Drop-in flush

Hinged up

Hinged down

Attic access traps

Openings made in the ceiling will encourage the flow of water vapor into the attic space. This can increase the risk of condensation, especially if the attic is not well ventilated. Attic access traps are made with seals to overcome this problem. Each trap has a molded frame that, when installed in a ceiling opening (as described above), forms a seal with the ceiling all around. It also

neatly covers the cut edges of the hole. The insulated trapdoor incorporates a flexible vapor seal between it and the hatch frame. There are hinged trapdoors and lift-out ones. Some are fire-resistant.

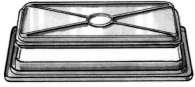

Frame and insulated trap form an airtight seal

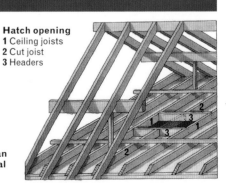

Hatch opening
1 Ceiling joists
2 Cut joist
3 Headers

19

Interior wall finish

As popular interest in authentic restoration of older houses grows, there is a new appreciation for the qualities of a plaster wall finish. While drywall is generally faster, easier, and cheaper to apply, plaster walls have a look and feel that is unmistakable to the discerning eye and sound-reduction properties that are superior to drywall. In the following pages you'll find both traditional and contemporary approaches to the plastering process as well as the methods used for installing and finishing drywall.

Traditional plastering techniques

Traditional plastering uses a mix of plastering material and water, which is spread with a trowel over the rough background in one, two, or sometimes three layers. Each layer is applied with a trowel and leveled accordingly. When set, the plaster forms an integral part of the wall or ceiling. Traditionally, plaster has been applied over masonry walls or wood lath—thin wood strips spaced slightly apart that hold the plaster in place. Over time, metal and gypsum lath have replaced the old wood type. Plastering well requires practice before you can achieve a smooth, flat surface over a large area. With care, a beginner can produce satisfactory results, provided that the right tools and plaster are used and the work is divided into manageable sections. All-purpose, one-coat plasters are now available, which makes traditional plastering easier for do-it-yourselfers.

Gypsum drywall

Manufactured boards of paper-covered gypsum are used to finish walls and ceilings in modern homes. Using drywall eliminates the long drying-out process necessary for wet plasters and requires less skill to apply. The large, flat boards are nailed, screwed, or bonded to walls and ceilings to provide a separate finishing layer. The surface of drywall can be painted, papered, or covered with paneling boards. It can also be covered with a thin coat of finish plaster.

Traditional plastering *(right)*
The construction of a lath-and-plaster ceiling and a plastered masonry wall.
1 Brick background
2 Ceiling joists
3 Lath background
4 First plaster coat
5 Second plaster coat
6 Finish plaster coat
7 Molding

Drywall *(far right)*
The construction of a modern drywall and ceiling.
1 Block substrate
2 Furring or stud wall
3 Ceiling joists
4 Blocking
5 Drywall
6 Cove molding
7 Tape
8 Joint compound

Traditional plastering

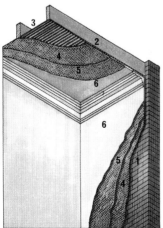

Drywall

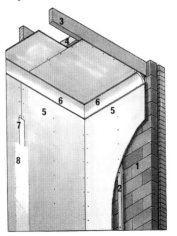

Plaster powder is normally sold in 50- and 100-pound bags. Smaller sizes, including 5-pound bags, are available for repairing damaged plasterwork. It is generally more economical to buy the larger sacks, but this depends on the scale of the work. Try to buy only as much plaster as you need—although it's best to overestimate slightly, to allow for waste and to avoid running out at an inconvenient moment.

Storage
Store plaster in dry conditions. If it is going to be kept in an outbuilding for some time, cover it with plastic sheeting to protect it from moisture. Keep the paper bags off a concrete floor by placing them on boards or plastic sheeting. Once opened, bags are more likely to absorb moisture, which can shorten the setting time and weaken the plaster, so keep an opened bag in a plastic sack sealed with self-adhesive tape. Discard plaster that contains lumps.

Premixed plaster
Ready-to-use plaster is sometimes available in plastic tubs. It's more expensive, but it is easier for most beginners to use and will keep for a long time, provided the airtight lid is sealed well.

Storing plaster
Keep an opened bag of plaster in a plastic sack sealed with adhesive tape.

Don't buy old plaster
Plaster can deteriorate if it is stored for more than three months. The paper sacks are usually date-stamped by the manufacturer. If you are buying plaster from a self-service store, choose the sacks with the latest date.

Plastering is carried out with modern gypsum plasters or mixes based on cement, lime, and sand. By varying the process and introducing different additives, manufacturers can produce a range of plasters to suit different substrates and different working conditions.

Plasters are basically produced in two grades: one for base or floating coats, the other for finishing coats. Basecoat gypsum plasters contain cement and lime and must be mixed on site with water and a lightweight aggregate, usually clean, sharp sand. Finish-coat plasters are ready for mixing directly from the bag and require only the addition of water.

Gypsum plasters

The majority of plasters are made from ground gypsum by a process that removes most of the moisture from the rock. This results in a powder that sets when mixed with water. Setting times are controlled by the use of retarding additives, which give each type of plaster a setting time suitable to its purpose. Gypsum plasters are intended for interior work only. They should not be used on permanently damp walls. Once they have started to set, don't attempt to add more water.

Plaster of paris

This quick-setting nonretarded gypsum plaster gives off heat as it sets. Either a white or pinkish color, it is mixed to a creamy consistency with clean water. It is unsuitable for general plastering, but good for casting, and can be used for repairs on decorative moldings.

Basecoat plasters

In traditional plastering, the finish is built up in two or three successive coats. Basecoat plasters are used for all but the last coat. Several types of basecoat plasters are available, some needing to be mixed only with water before application, and others that may need to

be mixed with sand or other aggregate before they can be used effectively. Which type you choose depends on the substrate, the specific job at hand, the need for economy, and the desired performance and working characteristics. It is crucial to read the package label to determine whether a particular formulation is suitable for the substrate or lath on which the plaster will be applied and to learn the best way to prepare the mixture.

Ordinary gypsum basecoat plaster, which must have sand or other aggregate added, is economical and suitable for most purposes. Wood-fiber basecoat plaster can be used, with the addition of water, only over wood, metal, or gypsum lath. But it must be mixed with sand for application over masonry. Wood- fiber plasters are about 25 percent lighter than sand and gypsum basecoats.

Special lightweight gypsum-based plasters, some premixed with the aggregate, are higher in strength than conventional plasters. These are commonly known by the trade names Structo-base and Structo-lite. Portland cement mixed with lime plaster is suitable for interior applications where a high moisture condition prevails and for exterior stucco work.

Gauging plasters

Gauging plasters are designed to be mixed with lime putty and applied as a finish coat. Some grades are harder and more abrasion resistant than others. In addition to blending gauging plaster with lime putty to improve workability, users sometimes add aggregate to roughen the finish texture.

Finish-coat plasters

Before the advent of modern gypsums, lime and sand for undercoats and lime for finish coats were employed in traditional wet plastering, often with animal hair added to the undercoat mix to act as a binder. Lime plasters are generally less strong than gypsum and cement-based plasters.

Lime is still used, but mainly as an additive to improve the workability of a sand-and-cement plaster or stucco. Most finish-coat plasters do not need to be mixed with lime putty. They are mixed with water only and are applied over compatible basecoats, gypsum lath, and moisture-resistant gypsum drywall. Some types are formulated for use over portland cement and lime basecoats in areas with moisture problems.

Molding plaster

With extremely fine grains and controlled set, molding plasters are preferred for casting and running ornamental trim and cornices. Sometimes lime putty is added to improve workability.

Patching plasters

A universal one-coat plaster can, as its name implies, be used in a single application on a variety of backgrounds and then troweled to a normal finish. The plaster is sold in 50-pound bags, ready for mixing with water. It will stay workable for up to an hour, and some types can be built up to a thickness of 2 inches in a single coat. Ready-mixed, one-coat plaster is also sold in smaller bags or plastic tubs. It is ideal for small repairs. All patching plasters are designed for high bonding strength.

Finish lime

Finish lime is added to plaster to provide bulk and plasticity to make it easier to spread. It also helps to control the setting time. Conventional finish limes must be slaked (saturated with water for 16 to 24 hours) to develop the desired putty consistency. Some specially processed types don't need to be slaked.

Other additives

Plaster retarders can be added to conventional plasters to slow drying to allow adequate working time. Accelerators can be added to speed up hardening when conditions require it.

Types of surface

Providing a key
Chop out loose mortar joints to help plaster adhere to the surface.

A well-prepared surface is the first step to successful plastering. New surfaces of block or brick may only need dampening or priming with a bonding agent, depending on their absorbency. Check old plastered surfaces for signs of damage. If the plaster is unsound (separated from the substrate), remove it and leave only stable material. Then treat the surface and replaster the damaged area.

Surface preparation

Brush down the surface of a masonry substrate in order to remove loose particles, dust, and efflorescent salts. Test the absorption of the background by splashing water on it. If it stays wet, you can consider the surface normal. This means that it will require only light dampening with clean water prior to applying the plaster.

A dry surface that absorbs the water immediately will take too much water from the plaster, so it is difficult to work. It will also prevent the plaster from setting properly and may cause cracking. If the masonry is dry, soak it with clean water, applied with a brush.

Remove loose particles with stiff brush

Highly absorbent surfaces

For very absorbent surfaces, such as concrete blocks, prime the surface with 1 part PVA (polyvinyl acetate) bonding agent and 5 parts clean water. When it is dry, apply a bonding coat of 3 parts bonding agent and 1 part water. Apply the plaster when the bonding coat is tacky.

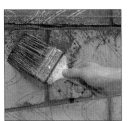

Prime porous surfaces to control too-rapid drying

Water-resistant surfaces

Prime smooth brickwork or concrete that is water-resistant with a solution of 1 part bonding agent to 5 parts water. Allow to dry, then apply a coat of 3 to 5 parts bonding agent to 1 part water and trowel on the plaster when the bonding coat is tacky. Alternatively, allow the surface to dry for no more than 24 hours before plastering.

A bonding agent improves adhesion

Nonabsorbent surfaces

Glazed tiles and painted walls are classed as nonabsorbent, and so will require a coating of undiluted bonding agent to enable the plaster to stick. The plaster is applied while the agent is tacky. For glazed tiles, an alternative is to apply a slurry of 2 parts sharp sand and 1 part cement, mixed with a solution of 1 part bonding agent and 1 part water. Apply the slurry with a stiff-bristle brush to form a stippled coating. Allow it to dry for 24 hours before plastering.

Smooth tiles can be keyed with slurry

You can mix plaster in any convenient container or dish. But it's easier to work with lightweight boards, which will allow you to carry the plaster around the worksite.

Mixing and carrying plaster
You can use ¼-inch exterior-grade plywood to make a useful board for mixing and carrying filler. Cut out a 1-foot square with a projecting handle, or make a thumb hole as in an artist's palette. Seal the surface with varnish, or apply a plastic laminate for a smooth finish.

Mortarboards
Mix plaster in a large plastic tray, or cut a piece of exterior-grade plywood, ¼ inch thick, to make a mortarboard about 3 feet square. Round off the corners and chamfer the edges all around. Screw three lengths of 1 x 2 furring strips (spaced evenly) to the underside of the board.

Using a stand
To help you pick up the mixed plaster easily, use a stand that will support the mortarboard at table height—about 30 inches from the floor.

To construct a folding stand, use 2 x 2 lumber for the legs and 1 x 2 furring for the rails. Make one of the leg frames fit inside the other, and bolt them securely together at the center.

Or you can use a portable folding bench (like a Workmate) to support the board. Just hold the middle support in the table's vise jaws.

Having prepared the surface, the next step is to mix up the plaster. Mixing plaster can be a messy job, so spread canvas drop cloths, plastic dust sheets, or old newspapers across the floor where you are working, and remember to wipe your feet when leaving the room.

Plaster that is mixed to the correct consistency will be easier to apply. Use a plastic bucket to measure the materials accurately. For large quantities of plaster, simply multiply the number of bucket measures; for small quantities, use half-bucket measures or less.

Old gypsum plaster stuck to your tools or equipment can shorten the setting time and reduce the strength of newly mixed plaster. Discard plaster that has begun to set and make a fresh batch. Mix only as much plaster as you will need. For larger areas, mix as much as you can apply in about 20 minutes.

Mixing undercoat plasters

Mix basecoat plasters in a plastic tray or on a mortarboard (see opposite). Measure out each of the materials and thoroughly dry-mix them with a trowel. Make a well in the heaped mix and pour in some clean water. Then turn in the dry material, adding water to produce a thick, creamy consistency.

Just add water to premixed gypsum plasters, which already contain an aggregate. Mix them in a similar way. Always wash down the tray or board after you have finished using it. You can mix small quantities of this type of plaster in a bucket. Pour the plaster into the water and stir to a creamy consistency; 2½ pounds of plaster will need about 1½ pints of water.

Mixing finish plaster

Mix finish plaster in a clean plastic bucket. Pour no more than 4 pints of water into the bucket, then sprinkle the plaster into the water and stir it with a piece of scrap wood or a paint stick until it reaches a thick, creamy consistency. Tip the plaster out onto a clean, damp mortarboard, ready for use. Wash out the bucket.

Mixing patching plaster

Pour out a small amount of patching plaster onto a flat board. Form a hollow in the center with your filling knife and pour in water. Gradually drag the powder into the center until it absorbs all the water, then stir the mix to a creamy thickness. If it seems too runny, add a little more powder. To fill deep holes and cracks, begin with a stiff mix but finish off with creamy mix.

Bonding agents are used to modify the absorption of the surface or improve the adhesion of the plaster. When using a bonding agent, don't apply a basecoat plaster any thicker than ⅜ inch at a time. If you need to build up the thickness, scratch the surface of the plaster to provide an extra key, and allow at least 24 hours between coats.

Bonding agents can be mixed with plaster or with sand and cement to fill cracks. Remove any loose particles and then use a brush to apply a priming coat of 1 part agent to 3 to 5 parts water. Mix the plaster or sand and cement to a stiff consistency, using 1 part bonding agent to 1 part water. Apply the filler with a trowel, pressing it well into the cracks.

Clean up as you go
Wash tools and brushes thoroughly in clean water. On a large job, it may be necessary to rinse out your brushes as the work progresses.

COVERAGE OF GAUGED-LIME FINISH PLASTERS				
Plaster product	Ratio of mix			Average coverage in sq. yds. per 100 lbs. of plaster
	Lime	Gauging	Sand	
Standard gauging plasters	2	1	—	19.5
	2	1	8	14
Structo-gauge	1	1	—	19
	2	1	—	21.5
Keenes cement	2	1	8	13.5
	1	2	—	18.5
	1	2	8	13.5

COVERAGE OF BASECOAT PLASTERS				
Plaster product	Mix	Approximate coverage in sq. yds. per 100 lbs. of plaster		
		Gypsum lath	Metal lath	Unit masonry
Standard gypsum basecoat plasters	Sand	10.5	5.75	9.25
	Perlite	9.25	4.5	7.5
	Vermiculite	9	—	8.25
Structo-lite	Regular	7	3.75	6.75
Structo-base	Sand	8.25	5	7.6

Plastering techniques

Plastering can seem like an overwhelming task to the beginner, and yet it has only two basic requirements: The plaster should stick well to the surface and be worked to a smooth, flat finish. Thorough preparation and careful choice of plaster and tools should ensure good adhesion. But the ability to achieve a smooth, flat surface will come only after some practice. Most plasterer's tools are somewhat specialized, but their cost will be justified in the long term if you are planning several plastering jobs.

Picking up plaster

Hold the edge of your hawk below the mortarboard and use your trowel to scrape a manageable amount of plaster onto its surface (1).

Take no more than a full trowel to start with. Tip the hawk toward you and, in one movement, cut away about half of the plaster with the trowel, scraping and lifting it off the hawk and onto the face of the trowel (2).

1 Load hawk   **2 Lift plaster**

Using plasterer's hawk and trowel

Applying the plaster

Hold the loaded trowel horizontally, tilted at an angle to the face of the wall (1). Apply the plaster with a vertical upward stroke, pressing firmly so that plaster is fed onto the wall. Flatten the angle of the trowel as you go (2), but never let the whole face of the trowel push against the wall. This induces suction and pulls off the plaster.

1 Tilt trowel   **2 Apply plaster**

● **Using repair plaster**
For small repairs, you can use the ready-mixed plasters that are available in tubs. For shallow repairs, brush on a thick coat of repair plaster and smooth it level with the spreader supplied.

For deeper holes, use a repair plaster designed for treating damaged plasterwork, cement stucco, and masonry. This remains workable for up to 4 hours. Apply it with a plasterer's trowel and work it to a smooth finish. In this instance, you can sand the plaster smooth after it has set.

Leveling up

To repair a hole in a plaster wall, trowel plaster so it sits just over the surrounding surface. Then use a straight-edged board to level the surface. Hold the board against the original plaster and work it upward while moving it from side to side. Then carefully lift it away, taking the surplus with it. Fill in any hollows with more plaster from the trowel, then level the surface again. Allow one coat of plaster to stiffen before you smooth it with a trowel. For two-coat work, scrape back the edges slightly to provide a key for the finish coat.

Work board up wall to level surface

Finishing the plaster

Apply the finish coat over a gypsum plaster undercoat as soon as it has set. A cement-based plaster must be allowed to dry thoroughly. Dampen its surface in order to reduce absorption before applying the finish plaster. Paper-faced board can be finished immediately, without wetting.

Use a plasterer's trowel to apply the finish plaster, spreading it evenly to a thickness of about 1/16 inch (but not more than 1/8 inch).

As the plaster stiffens, brush it or lightly spray it with water, then trowel the surface to consolidate it and produce a smooth matte finish. Avoid pressing too hard or overworking the surface. Sponge off surplus water.

Spray plaster occasionally as you smooth it

Repairing damaged plaster

Everybody who works with plaster will at some time have to fill small holes and cracks as part of normal preparation work, and these should present few problems. But once you start tackling more ambitious jobs, like taking down walls or filling in openings where doors or windows have been removed, you will need to develop some of the professional plasterer's skills.

Plastering over openings

Filling in door and window openings requires substantial plasterwork for the walls to look right when you're done.

Begin by filling the opening with standard wood framing materials. Measure the opening accurately and build a small replacement wall to fit the space. Add a top and bottom plate to the studs, push the assembly into the opening, and nail it securely to the surrounding framing members. Cover the surface with gypsum lath so you have at least ¼ inch left for plaster across the entire surface. You can either use one-coat plaster or a two-coat system.

For one-coat plaster, mix the plaster in a tub according to the manufacturer's instructions. Tip the mixed plaster onto a dampened mortarboard. Then scoop some up onto a hawk and apply the plaster to the surface with a trowel. Work in the sequence shown above. Start at the bottom of each section and spread the plaster vertically. Work on each area in turn, blending the edge of one into the next. When the sections are done, smooth the whole area with a straight board, fill any hollows, and smooth again. Let the plaster stiffen for about 45 minutes, until finger pressure leaves no impression, then lightly dampen the surface with a sponge. Wet the trowel and give the plaster a smooth surface.

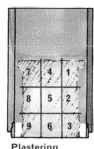

Plastering sequence

If using a two-coat system, apply the undercoat and finish coat of plaster as described above. Just be sure to scrape back the undercoat to a depth of 1/16 inch to allow for the thickness of the finish topcoat.

If damage to a corner extends along most of the edge, you can reinforce the repair with a metal or plastic corner beading.

Buy beading from a lumberyard or home center. Cut it to length with snips or a hacksaw. Metal beading has a protective galvanized coating; cut ends should be sealed with a metal primer before installing them.

Cut back the damaged plaster, wet the substrate, and apply patches of undercoat plaster on each side of the corner. Press the wings of the beading into the plaster patches (**1**), and use a straightedge to align its outer nose with both of the original plaster surfaces. Also check for plumb with a builder's level. Allow the plaster to set.

1 Press beading into plaster

Build up the undercoat plaster with your trowel until it is 1/16 inch below the old finished level (**2**). Apply the finish coat, using the beading as a guide to achieve flush surfaces. Take care not to damage the beading's galvanized coating with your trowel, or rust may come through later. To be on the safe side, brush a stain-bloking primer over the new corner after the plaster is dry.

2 Apply basecoat

Repairing a chipped corner

Repair damage to an external corner with one-coat or two-coat plaster, using a wide board nailed on one side as a guide to help you achieve a neat corner.

With a cold chisel, cut away the plaster near the damaged edge to create about a 3-inch-wide void on each side of the corner.

If using two-coat plaster, nail the guide board on one side of the corner, so that the board's edge is set back about ⅛ inch from the surface of the plaster on the other side of the corner (**1**).

Mix up the undercoat plaster. Wet the substrate and the broken edge of the old plaster, then fill one side of the corner up to the board's edge but not flush with the wall (**2**). Scratch the new plaster with the trowel to create a key for the second coat.

When the plaster has become stiff, remove the board, pulling it straight from the wall to keep the plaster from breaking away. The edge thus exposed represents the finished surface. To allow for the topcoat, scrape the plaster back about ⅛ inch, using the trowel and a straightedge as a guide (**3**).

Once the new plaster hardens, nail board in place before filling the second side of the corner with plaster. (**4**).

Let the undercoat set, then nail the board to the wall as before. But this time align its edge with the original plastered surface, and fill the recess with finish plaster. Dampen the undercoat to reduce the absorption. When both sides are firm, polish the new plaster with a wet trowel, rounding over the sharp edge slightly.

If you use one-coat plaster for the repair, set the guide board flush with the finished surface on each side.

1 Set board back

3 Scrape back edge

2 Fill flush with board

4 Fill second side

Repairing lath and plaster

Patching a drywall ceiling

When the plaster of a lath-and-plaster wall deteriorates, it often loses its grip on the lath. The plaster often bulges and may crack in places. It will sound hollow when tapped and tends to flex when you press against it. Loose plaster should be replaced.

Repairing holes in lath-and-plaster walls

Cut out loose plaster with a cold chisel and hammer (1). If the lath strips are sound, you can plaster over them.

After dampening the lath-and-plaster edges around the hole (2), apply a one-coat plaster, using a trowel. Press the plaster firmly between the lath (3), building up the coating until it's flush with the original plaster. Smooth it off with a straight board. Let the plaster stiffen, then smooth it with a damp sponge and a trowel. You can also apply the plaster in two coats. Scratch the first coat (4) and let it set, then apply the second coat and finish as before.

For larger repairs, use two coats of lightweight undercoat plaster, followed by a compatible finish plaster. For a small repair, press drywall joint compound onto and between the lath.

If lath strips are damaged, cut them out and either replace them, using metal mesh, or cover the studs with drywall and finish with plaster.

1 Cut away loose or damaged plaster

3 Apply plaster, pressing it between lath

2 Dampen edges of old, sound plaster

4 Scratch undercoat

Repairing a ceiling

A leaking roof or pipe above a lath-and-plaster ceiling can cause localized damage to the plaster. Repair the ceiling with an undercoat plaster, finishing with a topcoat plaster.

Carefully cut back the damaged plaster to sound material. Dampen the lath and the plaster edges and apply the undercoat (1). Don't build up a full thickness. Scratch the surface and let it set. Give the ceiling a second coat, then scrape it back ⅛ inch below the surface and lightly scratch it. When it has set, apply a finish coat (2).

1 Apply thin first coat with firm pressure

2 Level topcoat over previous undercoat

A misplaced foot in the attic, a roof leak that has gone unnoticed, a leaking water pipe—any of these can damage a drywall ceiling. Fortunately, serious damage is usually localized and is easily repaired.

2 Cut an opening

3 Nail in blocks

4 Nail in furring

1 Check for wiring and joists

Before starting work, turn off the electricity supply at the service panel. Next, check the direction in which the ceiling joists run and whether there is any electrical wiring close to the damaged area. If there's a floor above, you will probably be able to lift a floorboard to inspect the damaged ceiling. Or use a hammer to knock a hole through the center of the damage. You can look through the hole with the help of a flashlight and a mirror (1).

Mark out a square or rectangle on the ceiling, enclosing the damaged area. Then cut away an area of the drywall slightly larger than the damage, working up to the sides of the nearest joists (2). Use a drywall saw or a utility knife to make the cut.

Cut and toenail 2 x 4 blocking between the joists at the ends of the cutout. Make sure that half the thickness of the blocking projects beyond the cut ends of the drywall to serve as backing (3). Then nail 1 x 2 furring to the sides of the joists, flush with their bottom edges (4).

Cut a piece of drywall (the same thickness as the drywall in place) to fit the opening. Leave about a ⅛-inch gap all around. Nail the patch to the blocking and the furring, then fill and tape over the joints to give a flush surface.

Dealing with minor damage

It is not necessary to patch a ceiling that has only minor damage. Eliminate the source of the problem (if the ceiling is damp, let it dry out completely), then use drywall joint compound to make any repairs.

Decorative molding

Most distinctive older houses have molded plaster cornices and centerpieces in the main rooms. In comparatively recent times, when they became less fashionable, many of these ceilings were destroyed. Today, thanks to renewed appreciation of period plasterwork, damaged moldings are frequently restored or replaced.

Restoring original centerpieces

A ceiling rose, or centerpiece, is a decorative plaster molding placed at the center of a ceiling, usually with a pendant light fitting hanging from it. Original moldings of this kind are often caked with many layers of old paint that mask the fine detail. Restore them, whenever possible, by cleaning away the layers of old paint and repairing any cracks and chipped details with plaster or joint compound.

Fine detail can be obscured by paint

Installing a reproduction centerpiece

Replace an original ceiling molding that is beyond repair with one of the excellent reproduction moldings made from fibrous plaster. They are available in a range of sizes and period styles.

If there's a light fitting attached to the ceiling, turn off the power supply at the service panel, then disconnect and remove the entire fixture.

Use a hammer and cold chisel to carefully chip the old, damaged molding back to the ceiling plaster. Coat the surface with plaster, then let it dry.

To determine the exact center of the ceiling, stretch lengths of string from corner to corner diagonally. The point where they cross is the center. Mark the center point and drill a hole for the lighting cable. If the new centerpiece lacks a hole for a lighting cable, drill one through its center.

Apply a ceramic tile adhesive to the back of the molding, then pass the cable through the hole in the center and press the molding firmly into place. On a flat ceiling, the adhesive should be sufficient to hold the molding in place, but as a precaution, prop it until the adhesive sets.

Reinforce larger plaster moldings with brass screws driven into the joists above. Cover the screwheads with finish plaster or joint compound, following the contours of the molding. Wipe off surplus adhesive from around molding edges with a damp brush or sponge. When the adhesive has set, attach the light fixture. You may need longer screws to reach through the new molding.

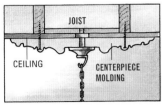

Reinforce larger moldings with screws

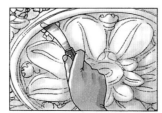

Cover screws, using putty knife

If it is ignored, sagging plaster on a traditional ceiling can develop into an expensive repair job, requiring the services of a professional. But if an area of plaster has broken away from its lath background and is otherwise intact, it can be reattached and prevented from collapsing.

Use galvanized or plated screws and washers

Screw repair

First lift the sagging portion of the ceiling, using wide boards propped in place with lengths of 1 x 4s or 2 x 4s.

Drive countersunk screws, fitted with galvanized or plated washers, through the plaster and into the ceiling joists. The washers should be about 1 inch in diameter, and they should be spaced about 12 inches apart. The screwheads will bed themselves into the plaster and can then be concealed with finish plaster or joint compound.

Plaster repair

A laborious but more substantial repair to a sagging ceiling can be made by using plaster of paris to bond the plaster back to the laths.

After propping up the ceiling as described for the screw repair, lift the floorboards in the room above (usually this is not necessary in an attic), so that you can get at the back of the ceiling. Use a vacuum cleaner to remove dust and loose material. If the lath and the old plaster is not clean, the plaster of paris will not adhere properly.

Wet the back of the ceiling with clean water. Then mix the plaster of paris in a bowl to a creamy consistency and spread it fairly quickly over the whole of the damaged area, covering both the lath and the plaster between the lath.

Although plaster of paris sets very quickly, it's best to leave the props in place until it has dried hard.

Spread plaster over lath and old plaster

Plastering a wall

Plastering a complete wall is not usually a job most homeowners will tackle. For new work, it's just easier and cheaper to use drywall. But sometimes there are large areas of damaged plaster that you want to repair with plaster, not drywall. These jobs can be done by nonprofessionals, but they will likely take you longer. The key to success is to divide the area into manageable sections.

Applying the plaster

Use a plasterer's trowel to scrape some plaster onto a hawk, and start the undercoat plastering at the top of the wall. Holding the trowel at an angle to the face of the wall, apply the plaster with vertical strokes. Work from right to left if you are right-handed; if you're left-handed, work from left to right.

Using firm pressure to ensure good adhesion, apply a thin layer first, then follow it with more plaster, building up to the required thickness. If the final thickness of the plaster needs to be greater than ⅜ inch, key the surface with a scratcher. Let it set, then apply a second or floating coat.

Fill the area between two screed boards (see sidebar right), but there's no need to pack the plaster tightly up against them. Smooth the surface with a straight board laid across the screed boards, sliding the board from side to side as you work upward from the bottom of the wall. Fill in any hollows, and then smooth the plaster again. Scratch the surface lightly, to provide a key for the finishing coat, and let the plaster set. Work along the entire wall in this way, and then remove the screed boards. Fill the gaps, smoothing the plaster with the straight board or trowel.

With gypsum plasters, the finish coat can be applied as soon as the undercoat is set. Cement undercoats must be left to dry out for at least 24 hours to allow for shrinkage. Wet them before applying the topcoat.

The order for applying plaster by a right-handed person.
Applying the topcoat left to right tends to even out any irregularities in the undercoats.

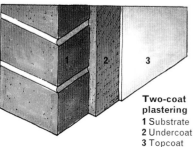

Two-coat plastering
1 Substrate
2 Undercoat
3 Topcoat

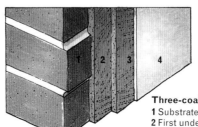

Three-coat plastering
1 Substrate
2 First undercoat
3 Second undercoat
4 Topcoat

Plaster layers
Plaster is applied in layers to build up a smooth, level surface. Three coats may be required on an irregular surface.

Cover the floor with a drop cloth. Don't try to reuse dropped plaster as it can contaminate fresh plaster.

In addition to specialized plasterer's tools, you need a level and some planed softwood boards ⅜ inch thick. These screed boards are nailed to the wall as guides for smoothing the plaster. Professional plasterers form plaster screeds by applying bands of undercoat plaster to the required thickness. These can be laid vertically or horizontally.

After preparing the substrate, attach the screed boards vertically to the wall with drywall screws. The screws make it easy to remove the boards later. Drive the screws just below the surface of the boards so they won't interfere with the trowel. Space the screeds no more than 2 feet apart. Use the level to get them plumb, shimming them if needed.

Mix the undercoat plaster to a thick, creamy consistency. Use a small batch first. You can use larger amounts when you become more proficient with the process.

Finishing

Cover the undercoat with a thin layer of finish plaster, working from top to bottom using even, vertical strokes. Work from left to right, if right-handed (see left); if left-handed, work from right to left. Hold the trowel at a slight angle, so that only one edge is touching.

Make sweeping horizontal strokes to level the surface further. Use the trowel to smooth out any slight ripples. Wet your trowel and work over the surface with firm pressure to consolidate the plaster. As it sets, trowel it to produce a smooth matte finish, but don't overwork it. Use a damp sponge to wipe away any plaster slurry that appears. The wall should be left to dry out for some weeks before decorating.

Drywall

Drywall (gypsum wallboard) provides a quick and simple method of covering walls or ceilings. It offers good sound insulation as well as fire protection. It's easy to cut and to install, either with adhesive, screws, or nails.

A range of drywall panels is available at home centers and lumberyards. They are made with a core of aerated gypsum plaster, and covered on both sides with a strong paper sheet. Standard panels have a gray paper backing, and an ivory-colored facing paper, which is an ideal surface for paint or wallpaper. If you want to replicate a traditional plastered surface (perhaps to match an adjoining wall) you can also apply a skim coat of wet plaster to the surface of the drywall. The panels are made in a range of thicknesses and sheet sizes, with square-cut ends and tapered edges.

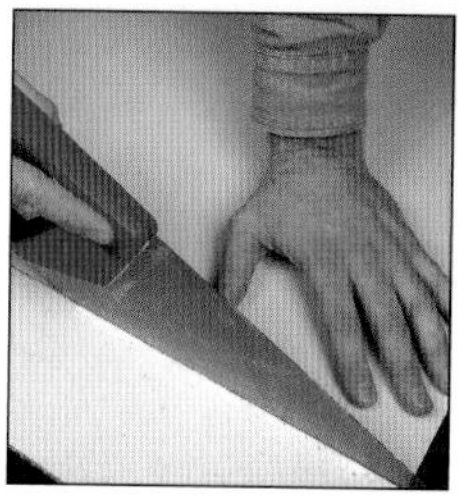

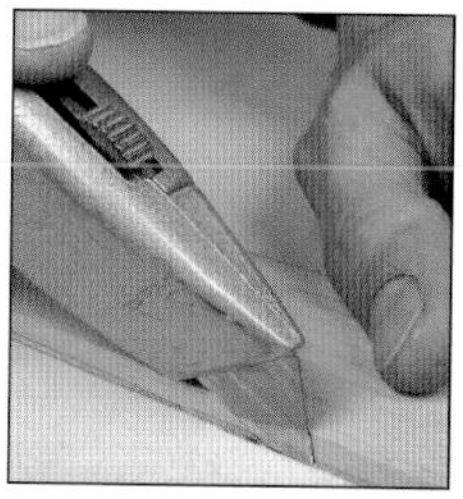

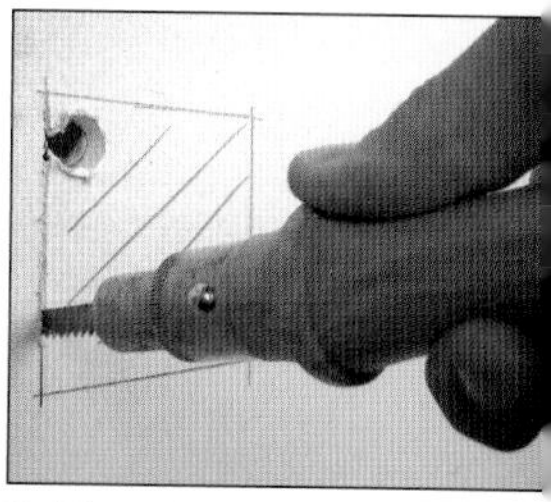

Cutting drywall
Cut the panels to size with a handsaw or a utility knife. Use a keyhole saw, drywall saw, jigsaw, or utility knife to cut any openings.

Storing and cutting drywall

Drywall is fragile, having very little structural strength. But despite its fragility, the sheets are quite heavy, so always get someone to help you carry them. Always carry vertically on edge. There is a good chance of breaking a panel if you carry it face up.

Manufacturers and suppliers store the boards flat in stacks, but this is usually inconvenient at home and isn't necessary for a small number of sheets. Store them on edge instead, leaning them at a slight angle against a wall, with their outside faces together to protect the finished surfaces. Stack the sheets carefully, to avoid damaging their edges.

Cutting drywall

You can cut drywall with a saw or with a utility knife. Support a sheet face-side up on boards laid across sawhorses. Mark the cutting line on it with the aid of a straightedge. When sawing the panel, hold the saw at a shallow angle to the surface. If the cutoff is going to be large, get a helper to support it as you approach the end of the cut, in order to keep the board from breaking.

When slicing plasterboard with a utility knife, cut through the facing paper and slightly into the material, using a straightedge. Then snap the board along the cutting line. Cut through the paper facing on the other side to separate the two pieces. Use a keyhole saw, jigsaw, or drywall saw to cut openings for electrical boxes and other obstructions.

After cutting, remove any ragged paper by smoothing the edges of the board with sandpaper or a coarse file.

GYPSUM PANEL PRODUCTS

GYPSUM PANEL TYPES AND USAGE	THICKNESSES (inches)	WIDTHS (inches)	LENGTHS (feet)	EDGE FINISH
Standard wallboard				
This material is generally used to finish walls and ceilings. The long edges of the panels are tapered to accommodate built-up layers of tape and compound used to finish joints. Available in a variety of thicknesses, ⅝- and ½-inch panels are typically used for single-layer applications direct to studs, while ⅜ inch is normally used over existing wall finishes; ¼-inch wallboard is generally used in multilayer applications for sound control and for curved surfaces with short radii.	¼ ⅜, ½, ⅝	48 48	8 8, 9, 10, 12, 14	Tapered
Water-resistant gypsum panels				
With a specially formulated gypsum-asphalt core and chemically treated face and back papers, this material is recommended for direct application to studs in bathrooms, powder rooms and utility rooms, to combat moisture penetration. Suitable as base for ceramic tile and plastic-faced wall panels.	½, ⅝	48	1, 10, 12	Tapered
Predecorated gypsum panels				
These are standard wallboard panels that have a wide range of factory-applied vinyl and fabric facings. Long edges of panels are beveled to form a shallow V-groove at joints.	½	48	8, 9, 10	Beveled
Gypsum-base panels				
Gypsum bases are used in conjunction with proprietary veneer finishes with less labor, weight, and residual moisture.	½, ⅝	48	8, 10, 12, 14	Square
Gypsum lath				
This product category includes a variety of panel products specially designed as a ground for standard plaster basecoats and finishes.	⅜, ½	16, 24	4, 8	Square

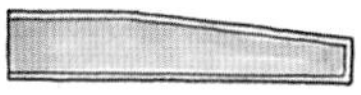

Tapered edge

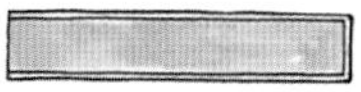

Square end

● **Types of edge**
Tapered edges are filled with joint compound and taped to provide smooth, seamless joints that won't show under a wall-covering or a coat of paint. Square edges need to be filled and taped, too, to ensure sound joints. But these butt joints are invariably more noticeable and so should be kept to a minimum.

Drywalling a wall

Drywall can be nailed or screwed to wood framing members of a stud partition or to wood furring strips that are fastened to solid masonry walls. If you're covering old drywall or plaster, the panels can sometimes be glued in place with adhesive.

Drywall panels can be installed horizontally if it is more economical to do so, but more often than not they are placed vertically. On ceilings, drywall panels should be installed across joists. All edges and ends of each panel must be supported by framing members. If you are finishing both ceiling and walls, make sure to cover the ceiling before you finish the walls.

Methods for attaching drywall

Attaching to a stud wall

Partition walls may simply be plain room dividers, or they may include doorways. If you are working on a plain wall, start installing the boards from one corner. If the wall includes a doorway, work away from the doorway toward the corners of the room.

Starting from a corner

Using a foot lifter (see below), hold the first panel in position. If necessary, mark and scribe the edge that meets the adjacent wall. Then fasten the board, securing it to all of the framing members (see fasteners at right).

Install the rest of the boards, working across the wall. Butt the tapered edges together, leaving a gap of about ⅛ inch between panels that will be filled later with joint compound. If necessary, scribe the edge of the last board to fit the end corner before nailing it into place. Cut the baseboard to length, scribe the end where it meets the existing baseboard, and nail the baseboard in place.

Starting from a doorway

Using the foot lifter, hold the first board flush with the door stud and mark the location of the top of the door opening on the front of the panel. From this point, draw a line 1 inch from the edge of the board to the top of the board. Cut out this strip to form a notch for the piece of drywall that will fit over the door. Push the panel back in place and nail or screw it to the wall.

Install the rest of the boards, working toward the corner. Butt the tapered edges and leave a ⅛-inch gap between boards to provide a key for the joint compound used to finish the wall. If necessary, scribe the last board to fit any irregularities in the corner before attaching it.

Cover the rest of the wall on the other side of the doorway in a similar way, starting by cutting a 1-inch-wide strip to create the other side of the notch above the door opening.

Next, cut a piece of drywall to fit above the doorway. Sand off any ragged paper at the edges before pushing the panel in place. Then continue installing the remaining panels on this side of the doorway as you did on the other side.

When all of the drywall is installed, tape and finish the joints, and spread joint compound over the nail- or screw-heads. When the finishing is complete, sand the compound with 120-grit paper, install the door and casings, and vacuum up all the dust. Then prime the walls for paint or paper.

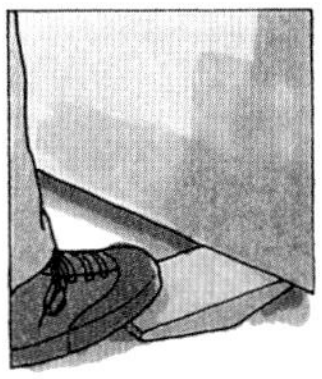

Using a foot lifter
A foot lifter is a simple device that holds the board against the ceiling, leaving both hands free for nailing. You can make one from a 3-inch-wide block of wood. Cut each drywall panel about ⅝ inch shorter than room height, to provide clearance for the foot lifter.

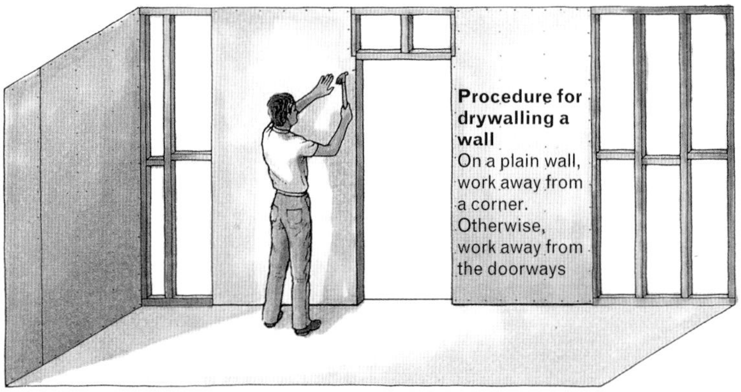

Procedure for drywalling a wall
On a plain wall, work away from a corner. Otherwise, work away from the doorways

Distances between stud centers
Standard wall construction has studs placed on 16-inch centers. The minimum drywall thickness for these walls is ⅜ inch, but most installers use ½-inch-thick panels. If the studs happen to be on 24-inch centers, you must use either ½-inch panels, or preferably ⅝-inch-thick panels.

Fasteners

These days drywall screws are the preferred fasteners for professional installers. But unless you've worked with them before, the nails shown below are easier for most people. Space the nails about 12 inches apart and no closer than ⅜ inch to the edges and ends. Drive the nails just below the surface, but don't tear the paper.

Board thickness	Nail length
⅜ inch	1 inch
½ inch	1½ inch
⅝ inch	2⅝ inch

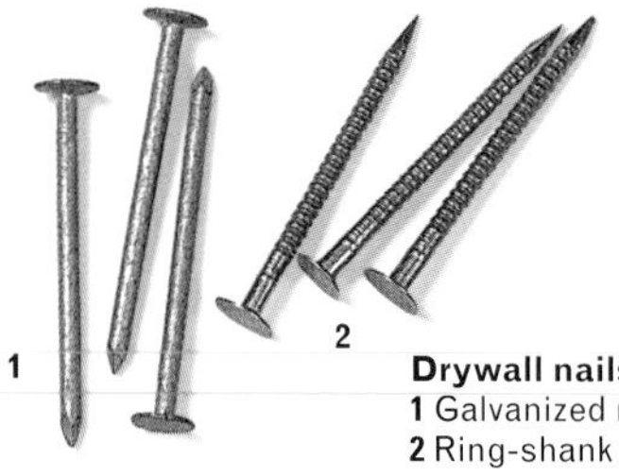

Drywall nails
1 Galvanized nails
2 Ring-shank nails

Drywall screws

Drywall screws do a great job of holding drywall panels in place. Screws that are 1¼ or 1½ inches long are used for typical work where a single thickness of drywall is being installed. Longer screws are available for multiple layers of drywall.

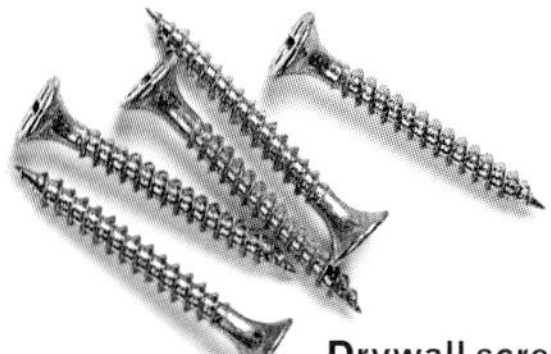

Drywall screws

Scribing drywall

If the inner edge of the first sheet of drywall butts against an uneven wall, or its other edge does not fall on the center of the stud, the board must be scribed to fit.

Scribing the first board

Begin by placing the first board in position (**1**). The illustration shows an uneven wall pushing the far edge of the sheet beyond the stud. Reposition the panel so that its inner edge lies on the center of this stud. Hold it at the required height, using a foot lifter, and tack-nail it in place.

With a pencil and a board cut to the width of the drywall panel, trace a line that reproduces the contour of the wall on the face of the panel (**2**). Make sure you keep the board level as you scribe down the wall.

Take the board down and use a utility knife or saw to trim the waste away. Cut on the inside of the scribed line, to leave a ⅛-inch gap next to the wall. Place the panel in the corner again, and attach it to the studs with nails or screws (**3**).

Scribing the last board

Temporarily tack-nail the panel to be scribed over the last installed panel (**4**), ensuring that their edges are flush with each other.

Using a guide board and a pencil, as above, scribe a line down the face of the top panel. Remove the marked panel, cut away the waste, then attach it to the studs (**5**). Fill and tape the joints, and cover the nail- or screw-heads with joint compound. When dry, sand all the joints smooth, vacuum up the dust, and prime the walls.

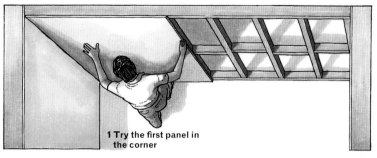

1 Try the first panel in the corner

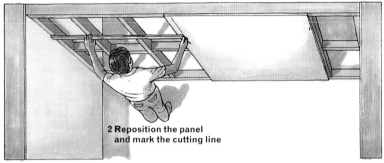

2 Reposition the panel and mark the cutting line

3 Cut the panel to size and nail it in place

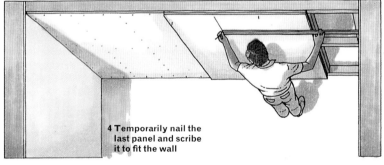

4 Temporarily nail the last panel and scribe it to fit the wall

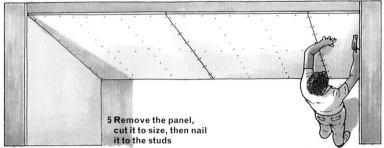

5 Remove the panel, cut it to size, then nail it to the studs

Drywalling a masonry wall

Drywall can't be nailed directly to masonry walls, so boards known as furring strips are used to provide nailing surfaces and to straighten out any unevenness on the wall surface. If the walls you are covering are in the basement, it's a good idea to use pressure-treated furring strips. You can install the strips directly over old plaster if it is sound. Otherwise, it's best to strip back to the substrate. If the wall is damp, treat the cause and let the wall dry out before starting work. Install any plumbing or electrical components before attaching the furring to the wall.

Layout

Using a straightedge and 4-foot level as a guide, mark the position of the furring strips on the wall. Place the lines 16 inches apart to create 16-inch centers for the drywall panels. The perimeters of windows, doors, and other openings all need to be covered with furring. The wall space above these openings needs furring too. Mark the wall for these pieces, making sure they fall on 16-inch centers, so the layout is consistent from one end of the wall to the other.

Attaching the furring strips

Cut the required number of 1 x 2 furring strips to length. Don't forget that the vertical strips will be about 3 inches shorter than the wall height to allow for the furring strips that fall across the top and bottom of the wall. Be sure to include any shorter strips that fall around and above window and door openings.

Nail the top and bottom strips in place first, using either masonry nails or cut nails. Then fill in between these strips with the vertical strips. Push each vertical strip tightly against the wall to see if it lies flat. You can correct irregularities in the wall by shimming out the furring strips with cedar shimming shingles. If you do install shingles at some point, nail the furring strip through these shingles to hold them in place.

Attaching the drywall

To attach the panels to furring strips, follow the procedure described for nailing to a stud partition. However, there's no need to notch the boards at the sides of windows and doorways, because you can place short furring strips just where you need them above the openings (see below). Follow the usual procedure for finishing the joints between the panels.

Cut the baseboard to length, and nail it through the drywall to the bottom furring strip. If you are using a high baseboard, the top edge should also be nailed to the vertical furring strips.

Shimming the furring strips

Masonry walls aren't always flat. Serious irregularities should be corrected so the finished wall surface is as flat and level as practical. You can do this by shimming out the furring before nailing the strips to the wall.

To check that the wall is flat, hold a long straightedge horizontally against it at different levels. If it is uneven, mark the wall at the points where it's most in need of adjustment **(1)**.

Hold a straight vertical board against the wall at any problem spot. Make sure this board is plumb and mark the floor behind the back edge of the board **(2)**. Draw a line across the floor connecting these marks **(3)**. Align all the furring strips with this line.

1 Check wall

2 Mark high point

3 Draw line on floor

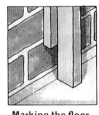

Marking the floor
Use a straightedge to mark the floor.

Attaching furring strips to a wall
1 Mark the positions of furring strips.
2 Attach horizontal strips.
3 Attach vertical strips.
4 Attach short pieces over doors and windows, offsetting them to avoid cutting notches in the panels.
5 Nail panels in place, beginning next to a door or window.

All joints between panels and any indentations left by nailing must be filled and sanded before the surface is ready for painting or wallpapering. You will need joint tape, joint compound, and a variety of specialized taping knives to get a high-quality finish.

Covering nails or screws

Fill the indentations left by nailing or screwing the panels in place. Use a drywall knife to apply and smooth the compound. When the compound has set, sand the surface flush with the surrounding panel surface.

Finishing tapered edge joints

Apply a continuous band of compound, about 3 inches wide, down the length of each joint. Press the joint tape into the compound, using a medium-size knife or a plasterer's trowel to smooth the tape in place and remove any air bubbles **(1)**. Apply another layer of compound in a wide band over the tape **(2)**.

When the compound has stiffened slightly, you can smooth its edges with a damp sponge, or allow it to set and sand it smooth with abrasive paper.

When all the filler has set, coat the joint with a thin layer of compound applied in a broad band **(3)**. Once this compound has set hard, lightly sand, then apply another thin but wider band over the first application. Feather the edges with the trowel or knife.

1 Press tape into compound

2 Apply compound in wide band

3 Apply thin but broad band

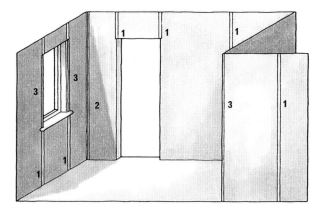
Finishing the joints
1 Use the tape flat for tapered and butt joints.
2 Fold the tape for insdie corners.
3 Use metal or plastic corner beads on outside corners.

Fiberglass tape can be used instead of traditional paper tape for finishing new drywall or for making small repairs. Because it has adhesive on the back side, this 2-inch-wide tape doesn't need to be embedded in joint compound. Just press it over the joint and then cover it with compound.

Applying the tape

Make sure that the joint surface is dust-free. If the edges of boards have been cut, sand them to remove all the rough paper.

Starting at the top, center the tape over the joint, then unroll it and press it in place as you work down the wall. Cut it to length at the bottom of the joint. If you have to make a seam in the tape, butt the ends, don't overlap them.

Cover the tape with compound, pressing it into the holes in the mesh. Smooth the compound so the mesh of the tape is visible. Allow the compound to set. Then, complete the joint with two more layers of compound, as described for paper tape.

Finishing butt joints

When a square edge butts against a tapered edge, fill the joint flush before you apply the tape **(1)**.

Where two square edges meet **(2)**, press compound into any gap between the panels and smooth it flush. When the filler has set, apply a thin band of joint cement to it and press the paper tape tight against the board. Cover this with a wide but thin coat of joint cement, then feather the edges.

Tools and materials
To finish drywall joints, you will need joint compound, a premixed plasterlike substance that comes in different size containers. The 5-gallon pails are the most common. The material is also available in dry form that is mixed with water on site. You also need some taping knives that range in width between 3 and 10 inches. To carry workable quantities of the joint compound around you need either a hawk or a drywall pan. To reinforce the joints you need paper or plastic mesh tape to embed in the joint compound. And, once the compound is dry, you need abrasive paper to smooth the joints.

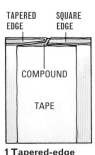
1 Tapered-edge joint

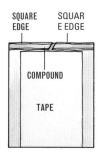
2 Square-edge joint

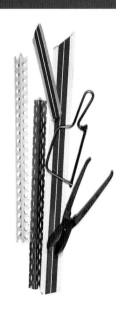

Finishing interior corners

Interior drywall corners are finished by a method similar to that used for flat joints. Any gaps are first filled flush with compound. Apply a band of compound about 3 inches wide on both surfaces. Make the surface as smooth as possible.

Cut the paper tape to length and fold it down its center. Then press the tape into the corner. Carefully run a small wood block or a 3-inch knife down each side of the joint to smooth and embed the tape, and to remove any air bubbles (1).

Cover both sides of the joint with a 3-inch-wide band of compound and feather the edges with a damp sponge or a taping knife (2). When the compound has set, apply a second, wider coat and feather the edges again.

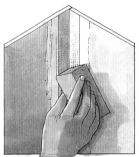

1 Smooth tape with wooden block or knife

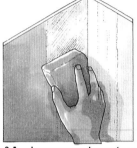

2 Apply compound over tape and feather edges

Finishing outside corners

Outside corners must be finished with a corner bead and compound to reinforce the joint. Plastic or metal beads are available for this job. If the corner is formed with one or two tapered edges, fill the tapers flush before installing the corner bead (1). Apply two coats of joint cement, feathering the edges as described for inside corners.

If both edges are square, then apply a thin coat of compound to both surfaces and install the corner bead (2). Be careful when you nail or screw the corner bead in place. It's easy to distort its shape by driving nails too deep or overdriving screws. Once the bead is distorted it's very hard to apply the top layers of compound so you get a smooth, straight corner.

Apply a second coat of compound to both sides in a wide band and feather it off with a knife or a damp sponge. When this coat is dry, apply two more coats of joint compound, feathering off as before.

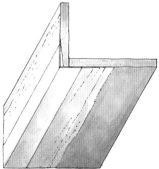

1 Fill tapered edge flush, then bed plastic bead

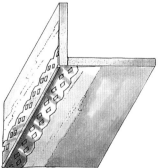

2 Embed metal bead in compound; feather edges

Having attached the drywall securely and finished the joints with tape and compound, now prepare the surfaces for paint or paper. This can be achieved with a thin coat of plaster applied with a trowel or by brushing on a coat of primer.

Finishing with plaster

If you don't want to apply paint or a wallcovering directly to the papered surface of the drywall, you can apply a thin coat of finish plaster instead. This may be necessary if you want to match adjacent plastered surfaces.

Applying a thin finishing coat is not an easy technique to master. Unless you are prepared to put in some practice, it is probably best to hire a professional, especially for ceilings. If you decide to try the job yourself, thoroughly study the section on plastering before you begin.

All the gaps and joints between the boards must be filled with compound and reinforced with tape, as described earlier, though in this case there's no need to feather the edges. The entire surface should be dry and the joints sanded smooth before applying the finish plaster.

Priming

Before drywall can be painted or wallpapered, it must be sealed with a primer. One coat of general-purpose primer evens out the absorption of the panels and the joint compound, and provides a sound surface for the wall finish. It also protects the panels if you steam-strip wallpaper in the future.

For small areas you can apply primer with a brush, but for anything over 10 square feet, a roller makes more sense. Just make sure the wall is dust-free before beginning.

Apply primer to even out absorption

Drywalling a ceiling

Drywall is the finish material of choice for just about all new ceilings, but it can also be used to replace or cover an old lath-and-plaster ceiling that has deteriorated beyond repair.

Any competent person can install the panels and finish them successfully. But the work is hard because the panels are heavy and it's always tiring to work over your head for long periods.

Preparing an old ceiling

Start by stripping away the damaged plaster and lath, and pulling out all the nails. Trim back the top of the wall plaster, so the edge of the ceiling drywall can be tucked in.

This is a messy job, so wear goggles, gloves, a respirator, and protective clothing while working. It is also a good idea to seal the gaps around the door, to prevent dust from escaping into the rest of the house. You will need to dispose of a lot of waste material, so have some strong plastic bags available and rent a dumpster.

Working on your own

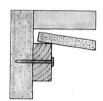

1 Support the boards with simple T-shaped braces called deadmen.

2 Nail a board to the wall to give temporary support to the long edge of the board.

3 Nail a temporary support board to the ceiling joists when butting boards.

Attaching drywall to the ceiling

Measure the ceiling area and select the most convenient size of panels to cover it. The panels should be installed with their long edges running at right angles to the joists. The butt joints between the ends of the boards should be staggered on each row and always supported by a joist.

Some people install ceiling panels working only from a stepladder. But this is difficult and cumbersome, especially if you haven't done it before. A better option for most people is to rent some interior scaffolding.

Nail perimeter blocking between the joists against the walls (if none exists), and for the best-quality job, install intermediate blocking in lines across the ceiling to support the long edges of the panels. If you decide to install intermediate blocking, use 2 x 4s or 2 x 6s and make sure their bottom edges are flush with the bottom edges of the joists.

Start installing the panels, working from one corner of the room. Full drywall panels are heavy material and it normally takes two people to support a large sheet while it is being nailed

in place (see below). However, if you have to work on your own, use support boards and T-shaped braces known as deadmen to hold the panels in place while you are attaching them (see far left). Make a pair of braces that are slightly longer than the overall height of the room **(1)**, using 2 x 2 lumber. Nail a crosspiece and a pair of diagonal struts to one end of each brace. Temporarily nail a 1 x 2 to the top of the wall to support the long edges of the first row of panels **(2)**. Support the next row with boards that overlap the edges of the first panels. Before you nail these support boards to the joists,

shim them with a thin board to provide the necessary clearance for the next row of drywall panels **(3)**.

Use nails or screws to attach each panel in place, working from the middle of each panel out to the edges. (Space the fasteners about 6 inches apart.) This prevents the panels from sagging in the middle, which is likely to happen if their edges are nailed first.

Cut the last panels in each row with a handsaw or utility knife, and do the same with the last row of panels in the room. Once everything is fastened in place, finish the joints as discussed earlier for walls.

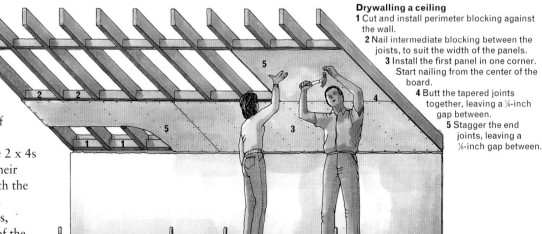

Drywalling a ceiling
1 Cut and install perimeter blocking against the wall.
2 Nail intermediate blocking between the joists, to suit the width of the panels.
3 Install the first panel in one corner. Start nailing from the center of the board.
4 Butt the tapered joints together, leaving a ⅛-inch gap between.
5 Stagger the end joints, leaving a ⅛-inch gap between.

Decorative wood moldings

Interior wood moldings, often called architectural moldings, are in part a legacy of the classic paneled walls found in grand houses of yesteryear. They include molded baseboards, chair rails, picture rails, and decorative cornice moldings. But moldings also have a functional purpose. They often cover up joints in wall finish, hide rough work, and protect the wall from daily abuse. Moldings are usually made from softwoods, and sometimes from hardwoods or even medium-density fiberboard (MDF) if they will be painted after installation.

Baseboards

Architectural moldings are both functional and decorative. A relatively high baseboard lends a period feel to a room and can cover up a lot of rough wall work underneath. By removing them you also have easy access to the wall cavities for such jobs as running new wiring. As a general rule, it's a good idea when choosing new molding to match the style of the other moldings in the house.

Chair rails

The chair rail provides a protective strip to keep the wall finish from being damaged by chairbacks. As such, it's most often used in dining rooms. But it can be used elsewhere too, wherever you want to establish a border between two different wall finishes—wainscoting on the lower part of a wall and paint or wallpaper above, for example.

Picture rails

Like other moldings, the picture rail was originally designed as part of ornate wood-paneled walls. It provided a strong ledge from which to hang heavy, framed pictures. These days picture rails are usually located about 12 inches below the ceiling, and serve a decorative rather than a functional purpose.

Cornice moldings

Cornice, or crown, moldings form a bold decorative feature where the walls of a room meet the ceiling. In old houses they can be made of plaster. But in newer houses, wood is almost always used.

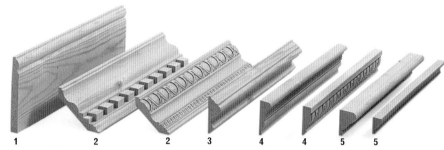

Types of molding
1 Baseboard **2** Crown or cornice **3** Large chair rail **4** Molded and carved chair rails **5** Small chair rails
Architectural moldings are decorative and functional

Making corner joints

Where pieces of molding meet at an outside corner, you have to miter the ends where they join. Cut miters using a handsaw and a miter box, or a power miter saw.

Where pieces meet at an inside corner, the joint has to be coped. To do this, first miter the end of a molding, then cut away the waste with a coping saw following the line formed by the mitered cut **(1)**.

For larger moldings that don't fit in your miter box, mark the profile on the back face, using a cutoff as a template **(2)**. Saw off the waste with the teeth of the coping saw facing backward, to prevent tearing out the wood fibers on the face of the molding.

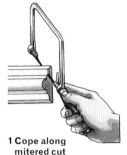
1 Cope along mitered cut

2 Use cutoff as template

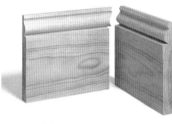
A baseboard with coped inside corner

Installing moldings

The best method for installing a molding will depend on the structure of the wall. On wood-framed walls, you can just nail through the molding and wall finish and into the framing members. On a masonry wall, you can use nails, expansion anchors, or plastic anchors. To install the anchors, lay out the wall first where the molding goes and drill clearance holes. Transfer the location of these holes to the molding and drill screw holes at these points. Screw the molding to the wall. In some cases, if the wall is very flat, you can use panel adhesive to glue the pieces of molding in place.

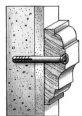
Masonry nail

Expansion anchor

Plastic anchor

Flooring is the general term used to describe the finished surface that is laid over a floor's structural elements, either floor joists or a concrete slab. The term "wood flooring" pertains to hardwood and softwood boards, or to any number of manufactured panels.

Floorboards

Hardwoods, like oak and maple, are generally used for making floorboards. The standard widths are from 1 to 3½ inches and thicknesses can range from a little as ⁵⁄₁₆ inch to as much as 2 inches. The standard thickness for tongue-and-groove flooring is ¾ inch and the most popular width is 2¼ inches.

Narrow boards produce superior floors, because any movement due to shrinkage is less noticeable. However, installation costs are high, so they tend to be used more in expensive houses. Softwoods, like pine and hemlock, are common in older homes but aren't installed often now.

The best floorboards are quarter-sawn **(1)** from the log, a method that diminishes distortion due to shrinkage. However, since this sawing method is expensive, floorboards are more often cut tangentially **(2)** to reduce costs. Boards cut in this way, however, tend to cup across their width and should be installed with the convex side facing up. The cut of a board, tangential or quarter-sawn, can be checked by looking at the annual-growth rings on the endgrain (see below right).

The joint on tongue-and-groove boards is not at the center of the edges but closer to one face. These boards must all be laid in the same way or the joint won't be flush. Although tongue-and-groove boards are nominally the same sizes as square-edged boards, the edge joint reduces their floor coverage by about ½ inch per board.

In some old buildings you may find floorboards bearing the marks left by an adze on the underside. Such old boards have usually been trimmed to the required thickness only where they sit over the joists.

Softwood and hardwood boards provide a durable floor that looks great when sealed and polished. Sheet materials such as flooring-grade plywood or particleboard are structural components, and are normally used as a subflooring for other more attractive floorcoverings.

Plywood

Any exterior-grade plywood can be used for subflooring. The panels are available with either square or tongue-and-groove edges. And they come in different grades. Usually one side of the panel is a better grade than the other. This side should be installed facing up.

If it is to be laid directly over the joists, plywood flooring should be ⅝ or ¾ inch thick. When it is laid over an existing floor surface—to level it or to serve as an underlayment for other flooring—it can be ¼ to ½ inch thick. Plywood panels and particleboard panels are laid in the same way.

Particleboard

Particleboard is made from adhesive-bonded chips of wood. Only flooring-grade particleboard—which is compressed to a higher density than the standard material—should be used for subfloors. You can buy either square-edged or tongue-and-groove panels that usually measure 4 x 8 feet and ¾ inch thick. Particleboard is less expensive than plywood and though it can absorb moisture, it doesn't delaminate in wet conditions the way that plywood can.

Medium-density fiberboard

Medium-density fiberboard (MDF) is a dense sheet material made from highly compressed wood fibers and glue. It is produced in different grades, and is suitable for subflooring where a plain, smooth finish is required. MDF is available in 4 x 8 foot square-edged sheets in a wide range of thicknesses. It is usually more expensive than particleboard, but cheaper than plywood.

Types of wood flooring
1 Square-edged softwood board
2 Tongue-and-groove softwood board
3 Square-edged particleboard
4 Tongue-and-groove particleboard
5 Square-edged plywood
6 Tongue-and-groove plywood
7 Square-edged medium-density fiberboard (MDF)

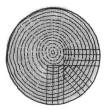

1 Quarter-sawn boards
Shrinkage does not distort these boards.

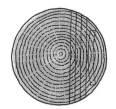

2 Tangentially sawn boards
Shrinkage can cause these boards to cup.

Lifting floorboards

Floorboards are rarely long enough to reach the entire length or width of a room, from wall to wall. If you have to remove a floorboard, the end joints between boards are the best place to start. If the board you need to remove has no joints in it, then start with a joint on an adjacent board.

● **Lift tongue-and-groove boards**
To lift a tongue-and-groove board, it is necessary first to cut through the tongue on each side of the board. Saw carefully along the line of the joint, using a dovetail or tenon saw held at a shallow angle. Having cut through the tongue, saw across the board and lift it as you would a plain, square-edged board.

Square-edged boards

Tap the blade of a cold chisel into the gap between the boards, close to the cut end **(1)**. Pry up the edge of the board, but try not to crush the one next to it. Push the chisel into the gap at the other side of the board and repeat the procedure. Ease the end of the board up in this way, then work the claw of a hammer under it until there is room to slip the chisel under the other side **(2)**. Proceed in the same fashion along the board until it is free.

1 Pry up board with cold chisel

2 Slide hammer and chisel under board

Lifting a continuous board

Floorboards are nailed in place before the baseboards are installed, so the baseboards will prevent you from lifting out a continuous board. You will have to cut the board in half before you can lift it out. Pry up the center of the floorboard with a wide cold chisel, until you can slip another chisel under it to keep the board bowed up. Remove the nails and, with a tenon saw, cut through the board **(1)** over the center of the joist. You can then lift the two halves of the board off the joists and away from the baseboards.

If a board is too stiff to be bowed upward or is milled with a tongue and groove, it will have to be sawn in place. This means cutting it flush with the side of the joist, rather then over the center of the joist.

To locate the side of the joist **(2)**, push the blade of a drywall saw into the gaps on both sides of the board. (The joints of tongue-and-groove boards will have to be cut beforehand.) Mark both edges of the board where the blade stops, and draw a line representing the side of the joist between these points. Make an access slot for the drywall saw by drilling three or four ⅛-inch holes close together near one end of the line.

Work the tip of the blade into the hole, and start making the cut with short strokes. When the cut is complete, pry up the board with a cold chisel, as described above.

1 Saw across board

2 Find joist's side

Freeing the end of a board

To release the end of a floorboard that is trapped under a baseboard, lift the board until it is almost vertical, then pull it straight out of the gap between the baseboard and the joist **(1)**.

A floorboard that runs beneath a partition wall must be cut close to the baseboard before you can raise it **(2)**. Drill an access hole so you can insert a keyhole saw blade or a floorboard saw blade **(3)**. Then carefully make the cut. Use shallow strokes to reduce the chance of hitting any obstructions underneath the floorboard.

1 Lift board clear

2 Cut close to wall

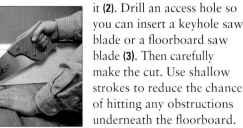
3 Use keyhole or floorboard saw to make cut

Refitting a cut board

The butted ends of boards should meet over a joist **(1)**. However, a board that has been cut flush with the side of a joist must be supported below when it is replaced. Cut a piece of 2 x 2 lumber and screw or nail it to the side of the joist, flush with the top edge. Screw the end of the floorboard to this support block **(2)**.

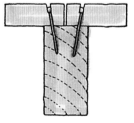
1 Boards share joist

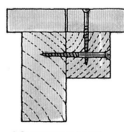
2 Support cut board

Replacing floorboards

Floors are subjected to a lot of wear, but it's usually water damage, fire damage, or wood decay that results in a floor having to be replaced. Before laying a new floor, measure the room and buy materials in advance. Leave the floorboards or sheet materials in the room you're working on for at least a week so the material can adjust to the temperature and humidity of the space.

Removing the flooring

To lift all the flooring, you must first remove the baseboards from the walls. If you intend to reinstall the same boards, number them with chalk before removing them. Lift the first few boards as described on the previous page, starting from one side of the room, then pry up the remainder by working a flat bar between the joists and the undersides of the boards. When lifting tongue-and-groove boards, carefully ease them up two or three at a time to avoid breaking the joints, then pull them apart.

Pull all the nails out of the boards and joists, and scrape any accumulated dirt from the boards and the joists. Make sure all the joists are sound and make any necessary repairs.

● **Closing gaps**
It is possible to reinstall floorboards without removing all the boards at once. Lift and renail about six boards at a time as you work across the floor. Finally, cut and fit a new board to fill the last gap.

Laying new floorboards

Although these instructions describe how to install tongue-and-groove boards, the basic method also applies to square-edged floorboards.

First lay a few loose boards together to act as a work platform. Measure the width or the length of the room, whichever is at right angles to the joists, and cut your boards to stop ⅜ inch short of the walls at each end. Lay four to six boards at a time. Where two shorter boards are to be butted end to end, cut them so that the joint will be centered over a joist.

Install the first board with its groove edge no more than ⅜ inch from the wall. Nail it in place with finishing nails that are at least twice as long as the thickness of the board. Use a nailset to drive the heads below the surface of the boards.

Finish the first row of boards, then start the next row by laying the first board so its groove slides over the tongue on the first-row board. For the joint to seat completely, the board being installed usually must be tapped into place. Don't strike the tongue with a hammer to do this. Instead, use a scrap block of flooring to cover the board tongue. Strike the tongue edge of the block to drive the floorboard into place. Continue using the scrap block to strike against as you work down the board. When the joint is tight, toenail the board to the joists by driving the nail into the corner where the top of the tongue meets the board. Set the nailhead. By nailing in this fashion (called blind nailing), the nails won't show when all the boards are in place.

When boards are too bowed to make a tight joint by driving them with a hammer and block, they must be wedged into place. To do this, nail a scrap board a few inches away from the bowed board. Then cut two wedges from scrap flooring and put them between the two boards. Drive the wedges together to force the board into place (**1**).

When you reach the far side of the room, cut the last boards to width and remove the bottom side of the groove so the board can drop into place (**2**).

1 Make wedges to drive boards tight

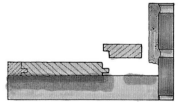
1 Make wedges to drive boards tight

Laying floorboards
Work from a platform of loose boards, and proceed in the following order:
1 Fix the first board parallel to the wall.
2 Cut and lay up to six boards, clamp them together, and nail.
3 Lay the next group of boards in the same way, and continue across the floor. Cut the last board to fit.

Floorboard clamp
This special tool automatically grips the joist over which it is placed by means of two toothed cams. A screw-operated ram applies pressure to the floorboards when the bar is turned.

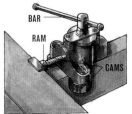

BAR
RAM
CAMS

Hire a special clamp to re-lay floorboards

Laying particleboard flooring

Particleboard is an excellent material for a floor that is going to be hidden under a finish flooring like vinyl or wall-to-wall carpet. It can be laid relatively quickly and is a lot cheaper than the equivalent amount of lumber flooring. It comes with square edges or tongue-and-groove edges.

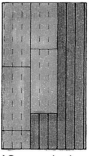

1 Square-edged sheets

2 T&G sheets

Laying out sheets

When using square-edged sheets **(1)**, run them in the same direction as the joists to keep the blocking to a minimum. When using tongue-and-groove sheets **(2)**, there is no need for blocking because the edge joint supports the sheets (see below).

Laying square-edged boards

Ring-shank nails
Nail down flooring sheets using 2-inch ring-shank nails, spaced about 12 inches apart.

Square edge

Tongue and groove

All the edges of square-edged sheet flooring must be supported. Lay the sheets with their long edges along the joists and nail 2 x 4 blocking between the joists to support the ends of the sheets. Nail blocking against the wall first. The blocking that supports the joints between sheets can be nailed into place as the sheets are laid.

Start with a full sheet in one corner and lay a row of sheets the length of the room, cutting the last one to fit as required. Leave an expansion gap of about ⅜ inch between the outer edges of the sheets and the walls. The inner edges should fall on the centerline of a joist. If necessary, cut the boards to width, but be sure to remove the waste from the edges closest to the wall, preserving the machine-cut edges to make neat butt joints with the next row. Nail down the boards, using 2-inch ring-shank nails, spaced about 12 inches apart along the joists and blocking. Place the nails about ¼ inch from the sheet edges.

Cut and lay the remainder of the sheets, with the end joints staggered on alternate rows.

Laying tongue-and-groove sheets

Laying square-edged sheets
The long edges rest on joists and the ends are supported by blocking.

Tongue-and-groove sheets are laid with their longer edges running across the joists. Blocking is required only to support the outer edges close to the walls. The ends of the sheets should be supported by joists.

Working from one corner, lay the first sheet with its groove edge about ⅜ inch from the walls and nail it in place. Apply construction adhesive to the joint along the end of the first sheet, and then lay the next one in the row. Make sure that the joint between the two sheets is tight. Nail the second sheet as described above, then wipe any surplus adhesive from the surface before it sets, using a damp rag.

Continue in this way across the floor, gluing all of the joints as you go. Cut the last sheet in the row. Then start the second row.

To get the grooves on the sheets in the second row to fit tightly over the tongues in the first row requires driving the two together. Slide the first sheet of the second row against the first-row sheet, place a scrap board along its long edge, and strike along the board until the joint is tight.

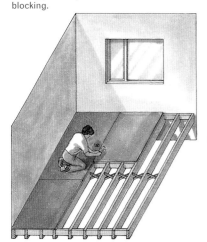

Laying tongue-and-groove sheets
Lay tongue-and-groove sheets across the joists.

Replacing baseboard

Baseboards are protective "kick boards" that create a decorative border between the floor and walls. Modern baseboards are relatively small and simply formed, with a rounded or beveled top edge. Repairing or replacing baseboards is sometimes necessary just from the wear and tear of normal living. But when you do any extensive remodeling, especially floor work, baseboard damage is inevitable.

In older houses baseboards are usually much bigger and often more ornate. Some lumberyards carry older-style baseboards, but generally they are hard to find. You can either make them yourself or hire a cabinet shop to machine them. Because replacing old baseboards can be time consuming, make an effort to preserve and repair older baseboards rather than discarding them.

Most standard baseboards are made of softwood, ready for painting. Hardwoods are not so commonly used; they are usually reserved for special decorative moldings and coated with a clear finish.

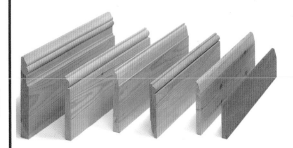

Selection of baseboard moldings
Most baseboards sold these days don't have much character. But a well-stocked lumberyard sometimes has a variety of more elaborate options including the types shown above. If you are unable to find baseboard to match your original, have one machined specially or make one from various pieces of standard moldings.

Removing the baseboard

Remove a baseboard by prying it away from the wall, using a crowbar or a flat bar. A continuous length of baseboard, with ends that are mitered into inside corners, may have to be cut before it can be removed.

Tap the blade of the crowbar between the baseboard and the wall, and pry the top edge away sufficiently to insert a thin strip of wood behind the crowbar, in order to protect the wall. Then pry out the baseboard again, a little to one side. Work along the baseboard in this way until the board is free. Having removed the board, pull the nails out through the back to avoid splitting the face.

Cutting a long baseboard
A long stretch of baseboard may bend sufficiently for you to cut it in place.

Pry it away at its center and insert blocks of wood, one on each side of the proposed cut, to hold the board about 1 inch from the wall **(1)**.

Make a vertical cut with a handsaw held at about 45 degrees to the face of the board **(2)**. Saw with short strokes, using the tip of the blade only.

1 Pry baseboard away from wall and block out

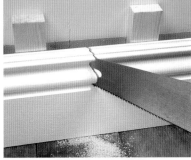

2 Cut through baseboard with tip of saw

Installing new baseboards

Whenever possible, restore a damaged baseboard, particularly if it has an unusual molding for which there is no modern replacement. If that's not possible, you could try to make a replacement from standard molding boards (see right), all of which are readily available.

Measure the length of each wall, bearing in mind that most baseboards are mitered at the corners. Mark the length of the wall on the bottom edge of the new board, mark a 45-degree angle

for the miter, and extend the marked line across the face of the board, using a square. Clamp the board on edge in a vise and carefully saw down the line at that angle, using a sharp handsaw.

Sometimes molded baseboards are scribed and butted at inside corners. To achieve the required profile, cut the end off one board at 45 degrees as for a miter joint **(1)**; then, using a coping saw, cut along the contour line on the molded face, so it will fit tightly against its neighbor **(2)**.

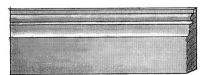

1 Cut 45-degree miter at end

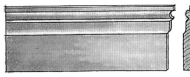

2 Cut shape following contour line

Doors: types and construction

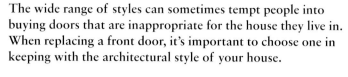

At first glance, there appears to be a great variety of doors to choose from—but most of the differences are purely stylistic and they are, in fact, all based on a relatively small number of construction methods.

The wide range of styles can sometimes tempt people into buying doors that are inappropriate for the house they live in. When replacing a front door, it's important to choose one in keeping with the architectural style of your house.

Buying a door

You can buy interior and exterior doors made from softwood or hardwood, the latter usually being reserved for special rooms or entrances where the natural features of the wood can be appreciated. Softwood doors are for more general use and most are intended to be painted. However, some people prefer to apply a clear finish.

Glazed doors are often used for front and rear entrances. Traditionally these feature wood-frame construction, though modern steel doors can be bought in standard sizes, complete with double glazing and numerous accessories.

Frame-and-panel doors are usually supplied in unfinished wood, so you can stain, paint, or clear-finish them to suit your taste.

Door sizes

Doors are made in several standard sizes, which meet most domestic needs. The two most common heights are 6 feet 8 inches and 7 feet. Widths usually start at 2 feet 2 inches and go to about 3 feet in 2-inch increments. Most residential doors are either 1⅜ inches or 1¼ inches thick.

Older houses often have relatively large doors to the main rooms, but modern homes tend to have the same size (6 feet 8 inches by 2 feet 6 inches) throughout the house, except for entrance doors, which most codes require to be 3 feet wide.

When replacing a door in an old house, where the openings may well be of nonstandard sizes, have a door made to fit the opening or buy a larger one and trim it to fit, removing an equal amount from each edge to preserve the door's symmetry.

Panel doors

Panel doors have a hardwood or softwood frame made with mortise-and-tenon or dowel joints. The frame is rabbeted or grooved to house the panels, which can be of solid wood, plywood, or glass. Doors constructed from hardboard, steel, or plastic panels are also available.

Flush doors

Most flush doors have a softwood frame faced with sheets of plywood or hardboard on both sides. Mainly used for interior doors, they're simple, lightweight, easy to hang, and inexpensive. Exterior flush doors have internal reinforcement blocks for lock hardware and mail slots.

1 Muntins
These are the central vertical members of the door. They are jointed into the three cross rails.

2 Panels
These may be of solid wood or of plywood. They are held loosely in grooves in the frame to ensure that they can move without splitting. They stiffen the door.

3 Cross rails
The top, center, and bottom rails are tenoned into the stiles. In some doors, the mortise-and-tenon joints are replaced with dowel joints.

4 Stiles
These are the upright members at the sides of the door. They carry the hinges and the lock.

Panel-door moldings
The frame's inner edges may be plain or molded to form a decorative border. Small moldings are either machined on the frame before assembly or machined separately and nailed to the inside edge of the frame. An ordinary recessed molding (see left) can shrink away from the frame and crack the paint. An overlay molding, which laps the frame, helps overcome this problem.

Recessed molding

Overlay molding

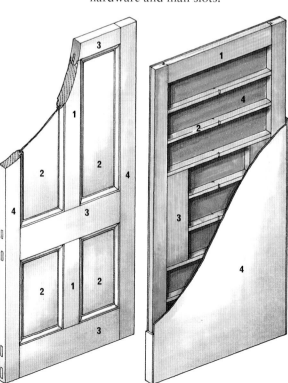

Panel door

Flush door

1 Top and bottom rails
These are tenoned into the stiles.

2 Intermediate rails
These lighter rails, joined to the stiles, are notched to allow the passage of air, in order to prevent mold growth.

3 Lock blocks
A softwood block able to take a lockset is glued to each stile.

4 Panels
The plywood or hardboard panels are left plain for painting or finished with a wood veneer. Metal-skinned doors may be ordered specially.

Core material
Paper or cardboard honeycomb is often sandwiched between the panels in place of intermediate rails.

Utility doors

These doors have a rustic look and are often found in old houses, outbuildings, attics, and basements. They are strong, easy to build, and when well maintained can last a very long time. These doors are usually hung with strap hinges.

1 Face boards
Tongue-and-groove boards are nailed to cross-rail boards.

2 Strap hinges
Long strap hinges are used to carry the weight of a large exterior door.

3 Braces
These diagonal boards, sometimes notched into the cross rails, keep the door from sagging.

4 Cross rails
These are the support boards that the face boards are nailed to.

Framed utility door

sic utility door

Exterior doors

An exterior door is installed in a heavy wood frame consisting of a head jamb at the top, a sill at the bottom that's outfitted with a threshold, and side jambs, which are usually joined to the other pieces with dado joints.

In old houses, a section of the floor framing may need to be notched to accept the sill. But in newer homes, prehung exterior doors are made to rest on top of the subfloor. Thresholds come in different styles and are designed to seal the bottom of the door from the elements while allowing it to swing freely.

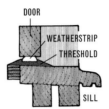

DOOR
WEATHERSTRIP
THRESHOLD
SILL

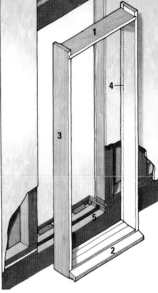

Exterior doorframe
1 Head jamb
2 Sill
3 Side jamb
4 Doorjamb rabbet
5 Notched floor framing

Interior doors

Interior doors are hung in frames that are similar to (but less sturdy than) those used for exterior doors. No sill is present, although in some cases a wood threshold may be added. Usually, interior doors come prehung (the door is already hung on the frame), and are installed with the frame as single units.

The head jamb **(1)** and side jambs **(2)** are fastened to the rough wall opening with shims **(3, 4)** to level and plumb the frame, and to space it evenly from side to side. If the space around the frame is small, wedge-shaped cedar shingles make excellent shims. They are held in place with finishing nails driven through the jambs and shims and into the studs at the sides and the header above.

There are many different styles of interior doors. Generally it's best to choose one that is the same or similar to the other doors in the house. Make sure the jambs on the door you choose are the same width as the thickness of the wall. If you can't find a frame that's a good match, you'll have to cut the jambs narrower or add extension strips to the edges of the jambs.

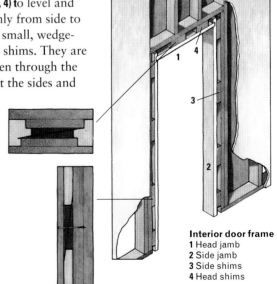

Interior door frame
1 Head jamb
2 Side jamb
3 Side shims
4 Head shims

Fitting and hanging doors

● **Measurements**
A door that fits well will open and close freely and look symmetrical in the frame. Use the figures given below as a guide for trimming the door and laying out the position of the hinges.

¹⁄₁₆ inch clearance at top and sides

Upper hinge 7 inches from the top

Lower hinge 10 inches from the bottom

¹⁄₄ to ¹⁄₂ inch gap at the bottom

Whatever style of door you want to install, the procedure is similar, with only minor differences. Two good-quality 4-inch butt hinges are enough to support a standard door. But a third, central hinge should be added to an exterior door or a heavy hardwood door.

You will have to try a door in its frame several times to obtain a perfect fit, so it is best to have someone working with you.

Installing a door

Before attaching hinges to a new door, make sure that it fits well in its frame. It should have a clearance of ¹⁄₁₆ inch at the top and sides, and should clear the floor by at least ¹⁄₄ inch; as much as ¹⁄₂ inch may be required for a carpeted floor.

Measure the height and width of the door opening, and the depth from the edge of the jamb to the doorstop molding. Ideally, choose a door that is the right size. But if you can't get one that fits the opening exactly, select one large enough to be trimmed down.

Cutting to size

New doors are often supplied with stile extensions that prevent the corners from being damaged while the doors are in storage. Cut these off with a saw (**1**) before starting to trim the door to size.

Transfer the measurements from the opening to the door, making allowance for the necessary clearances all around. To reduce the width of the door, support it on edge and plane the stile down to the marked line. If a lot of wood has to be removed, take some off each stile. This is especially important in the case of panel doors, in order to preserve their symmetry.

If you need to reduce the height of the door by more than ¹⁄₄ inch, remove the waste with a saw and finish off with a plane. Otherwise, just trim it to size with the plane (**2**), which must be extremely sharp to deal with the endgrain of the stiles. To avoid chipping out the corners, work from each corner toward the center of the bottom rail.

Supporting the door on thin wedges (**3**), try it in the frame. If it still does not fit, take it down and remove more wood where appropriate.

1 Saw off extensions

2 Plane to size

3 Wedge door

Installing hinges

The upper hinge is set about 7 inches from the top edge of the door, and the lower one about 10 inches from the bottom. They are cut equally into the stile and the doorframe. Wedge the door in its opening so it is properly aligned, and mark the positions of the hinges on both the door and the frame.

1 Mark around leaf with pencil

Stand the door on edge, hinge stile up. Open a hinge and, with its knuckle projecting from the edge of the door, align it with the marks and draw around the leaf with a pencil (**1**). Set a marking gauge to the thickness of the leaf and mark the depth of the recess. With a chisel, make a series of shallow cuts across the grain (**2**) and remove the waste to the scored line. Repeat the procedure with the second hinge. Then,

2 Cut across grain with chisel

3 Mark size of leaf on frame

using the leaves as guides, drill pilot holes for the screws and install both hinges into their recesses.

Wedge the door in its open position, aligning the free hinge leaves with the marks on the doorframe. Make sure the knuckles of the hinges are parallel with the frame, then trace the leaves on the frame (**3**). Cut out these recesses as you did the others.

Adjusting and aligning

Hang the door with one screw holding each hinge, and see if it closes smoothly. If the lock stile rubs on the frame, you may have to make one or both recesses slightly deeper. If the door appears to strain against the hinges, it is said to be hingebound. In this case, insert thin cardboard pieces beneath the hinge leaves to shim them out. When you're satisfied that the door opens and closes properly, drive in the rest of the screws.

Rising butt hinges

Rising butt hinges, which lift a door as it is opened, prevent it from dragging on a thick carpet. These hinges are made in two parts: a leaf with a fixed pin is screwed to the doorframe, and a leaf with a single knuckle is fixed to the door. The knuckle pivots on the pin.

Rising butt hinges must be installed one way up only, and are therefore made specifically for left-hand or right-hand openings. The countersunk screw holes in the fixed-pin flap indicate which side it is intended for.

Fitting the hinges

Trim the door and mark positions for the hinges (see opposite). But before installing the hinges, plane a shallow bevel at the top outer corner of the hinge stile, so that it will clear the frame as it opens. Because the stile runs through to the top of the door, plane from the outer corner toward the center, to avoid splitting the wood. The top piece of the doorstop will mask the bevel when the door is closed.

Install the hinges to the door and the frame. And then, taking care not to damage the trim above the opening, lower the door onto the hinge pins.

Left-hand opening   Right-hand opening

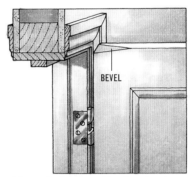

Plane shallow bevel to clear doorframe

Adjusting butt hinges

If a door catches on a bump in the floor as it opens, you can fit rising butt hinges to fix the problem.

However, it's sometimes possible to overcome the problem by resetting the existing hinges so that the knuckle of the lower one projects slightly more than the top one. The door will still hang vertically when closed—but as it opens, the out-of-line pins will throw the door upward, enabling it to clear the bump.

Resetting the hinges
You may have to reset both hinges to the new angle to prevent binding.

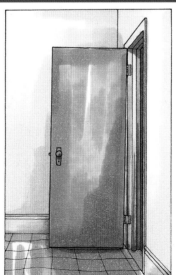

Installing a weatherboard

On some older houses, exterior doors don't have weather stripping installed and the sills are not outfitted with a watertight threshold. As a result, driving rain will be forced past the door and into the house. Of course, you can always replace an old door with a new one that comes with proper seals. But if you'd rather keep the door you have, you can create your own weather stripping.

A weatherboard is a molding that goes across the outside bottom edge of the door and sheds water that flows down the door away from the bottom of the door. To install one, measure the width of the opening between the doorstops and cut the molding to fit, shaving one end at a slight angle where it meets the doorframe on the lock side. This will allow it to clear the frame as the door swings open.

Use screws and a waterproof glue to attach the weatherboard to an unpainted door. When attaching one to a door that is already finished, apply a thick coat of primer to the back surface of the weatherboard to make a weatherproof seal. Then screw the weather stripping in place while the primer is still wet.

A door threshold should also have a weather bar installed as shown below. If the door is not typically exposed to driving rain, you can just install a weather bar and cut a rabbet in the bottom edge of the door that will seal against the bar.

Effects of weathering
A sadly neglected panel door that could have been preserved by applying a weatherboard before the deterioration had become widespread.

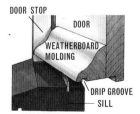

Door with a weatherboard installed

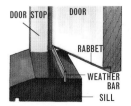

Sill outfitted with a weather bar

Casing molding

Casing moldings provide a decorative frame to a door, as well as concealing the joint between the doorjambs and the wall. The same moldings are used around windows. Standard casing moldings are stock items at lumberyards and home centers. But a variety of more elaborate casings are sometimes available if you have an architectural molding supplier in your area. If there's a particular profile you want to duplicate, you can have moldings made to order at some cabinet shops.

Reproduction casing moldings

Installing case molding

A classical casing treatment includes fluted molding along the sides and top of the door. At the bottom of the side casings, a plinth block is used to make a decorative transition between the casing and the baseboard in the room. At the top corners of the doorjambs, corner blocks are installed, partly for decorative purposes like the plinth blocks. But they also serve a functional purpose. They eliminate the need for miter joints where the side and top casing boards meet. Butt joints are much easier to install.

When casing a door, install the plinth blocks (**1**). Then measure the length from the top of the plinth to ¼ inch above the bottom of the top doorjamb. Cut the casings to this length and nail them into the jambs and the wall. Nail the corner blocks on top of the side casings (**2**), then cut and install the top casing between the corner blocks.

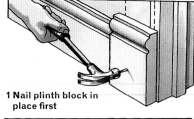

1 Nail plinth block in place first

2 Nail corner block on top of side casing

Installing standard casings

Hold a short length of casing molding about ¼ inch above the door opening, check that it's level, and mark its width on the wall. Next, hold one slightly long side casing board in place about ¼ inch from the edge of the doorjamb. Transfer the marks from the wall onto the casing board (**1**).

Cut a 45-degree miter on the marked end of the casing. Then nail it to the doorjamb, using 2-inch finishing nails driven every 12 inches. Don't drive the nails in fully at this stage, in case you need to move the casing. Cut and install the other side casing, using the same procedure.

Rest the top piece of casing upside down on the ends of the side casings and mark its length (**2**). Cut a miter at each end and nail the molding between the side casings and into the top doorjamb and the wall (**3**). Then line up the miter joints between the two boards, so the surface is flush, and drive a nail through the top casing into the mitered joint at both ends (**4**). Drive all the nailheads below the surface with a hammer and a nailset. Then fill the holes with wood filler, let the filler dry, and sand it smooth. Prime and paint. If you are planning to finish the casings with a clear varnish, fill the nail holes with a colored wood filler that closely matches the color of the wood.

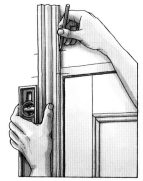

1 Mark length of side casing

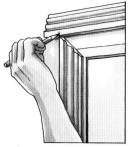

2 Mark length of top casing

If you are restoring an older house, you may find that the doorjambs are out of square and 45-degree miters will not fit tightly together. In this situation, hold each board in place with its inside edge parallel to the jamb and mark along the edges on the wall (**1**). Mark a diagonal line where the lines cross (**2**) to give the angle for the proper miter. Set an adjustable bevel to this angle and mark both casing boards with the bevel. Make the cuts.

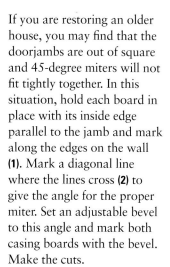

1 Mark parallel lines Hold each component in position parallel with the jambs and mark along the edges.

2 Mark the diagonal Where the lines cross, mark a diagonal line.

3 Nail top casing to top doorjamb

4 Drive nail into mitered joint

Door hardware

Installing a door knocker

A traditional set of exterior door hardware includes a mail slot, a doorknob, and a knocker. Of the three, the door knocker is probably considered optional by more people than the other two. From a functional point of view, electric doorbells have made door knockers obsolete. But as decorative hardware, knockers still have their place, especially in renovation work.

On a panel door, install the knocker to the muntin at about shoulder height. Mark a vertical centerline on the muntin at the required height and drill a clearance hole for the mounting screw or screws. Attach the knocker according to the manufacturer's instructions.

Reproduction brass fittings are usually finished at the factory with a clear lacquer to prevent tarnishing. If yours is not, apply a clear acrylic lacquer yourself.

Choose hardware to suit door style

Installing a mail slot

Mail slots are available in a variety of styles and materials—solid brass, stainless steel, plated brass, cast iron, and aluminum. They are designed either for horizontal or for vertical installation. Installing a horizontal mail slot is shown here. But the same methods apply to the vertical type installed in the door stile.

Mark out the rectangular opening on the center of the cross rail. The slot must be only slightly larger than the hinged flap on the outside (**1**). Drill a ½-inch access hole in each corner of the rectangle for the blade of a keyhole saw or a power jigsaw. After cutting out the slot, trim the corners with a chisel and clean up the edges.

Mark and drill the mounting holes, then attach the mail slot (**2**). You may have to shorten the screws if the door is thin. Plug or fill the counterbored holes that house the screwheads.

Better still, install an internal flap cover. These are held in place with small woodscrews. A flap cover reduces drafts, has a neat, finished appearance, and allows you to remove the mail-slot hardware easily for repairs or replacement.

1 Sizing the opening
Take dimensions from the flap and make the opening slightly larger

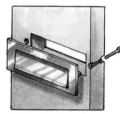

2 Counterbore door for plate and bolts

Installing hand plates
Designed to protect the paint on interior doors, hand plates are screwed to each side of the lock stile, just above the center rail.

Installing a doorknob

A period doorknob, whether wrought iron or brass, can be an attractive feature on just about any door. Such knobs are reproduced in many traditional styles and patterns.

A doorknob, often called a pull to differentiate between it and a lockset, is usually installed on the center of the lock stile, at the height of the door's cross rail. But personal preference plays a role here. Some people install them higher on the stile or in the middle of the cross rail.

Drill a counterbored hole from the back side of the door for the head of the screw that holds the knob. The clearance hole for the screw shank passes right through the door.

Hold the backplate and knob on the door, then insert and tighten the screw. For a neat finish, plug the screw hole on the back side of the door to conceal the screwhead.

Counterbore hole for fixing screw

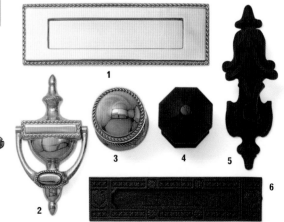

Reproduction door hardware
1 Brass mail-slot plate   **4** Wrought-iron doorknob
2 Brass knocker   **5** Wrought-iron knocker
3 Brass doorknob   **6** Wrought-iron mail-slot plate

Windows: types and construction

The purpose of any window is to allow natural light into the house and to provide ventilation. Traditionally, windows were referred to as "lights," and the term "fixed light" is still used to describe a window or part of a window that doesn't open. The part of a window that opens is called a sash. The sash can slide up and down or side to side in tracks or can be hinged on the side or the top. Windows with side-hinged sashes are usually called casement windows. Window sashes can also pivot, and a group of smaller glass panes can be operated together to form a jalousie window.

Most window frames and sashes are made of solid wood. In many cases, the outside surfaces are clad with painted aluminum or colored vinyl.

● **Window frames**
Most frames and sashes are made up from molded sections of solid wood. However, mild steel, aluminum, and rigid plastic are also used.

1 Casement window

2 Glazing bars

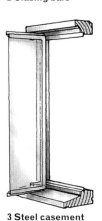

3 Steel casement

Casement windows

One of the more common windows is the simple hinged or casement window. Traditional versions are made of wood, and are fabricated much like doors. Vertical side jambs are joined to a head jamb at the top and a sill at the bottom (see below). Depending on the size of the window, the frame is sometimes divided vertically by a mullion with another side-hinged casement on the other side, or horizontally by a transom (1) and an awning window.

A side-hung casement sash is attached with either a continuous hinge or with butt hinges. A lever handle, sometimes called a "cockspur," is mounted on the sash stile and is used for opening, closing, and locking the sash. A casement stay attached to the bottom rail holds the sash open in various positions. With a top-hung casement (or awning sash), the stay also secures the window in the closed position.

Glazing bars, lightweight, molded strips of wood, steel, or vinyl, are often used to divide the glazed areas of a window into smaller panes (2).

Mild-steel casement windows (3) have relatively slim welded frames and sashes. They are strong and durable, but will rust unless protected by galvanized plating or high-quality metal paint. Modern versions are galvanized by a hot-dip process, then finished with a colored polyester coating.

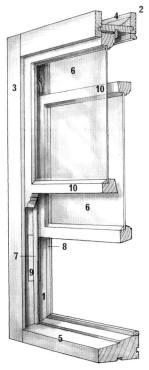

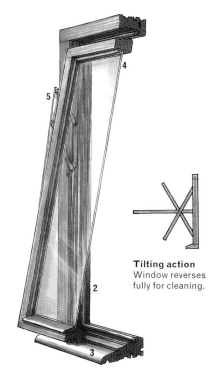

Tilting action
Window reverses fully for cleaning.

Casement window
1 Jamb
2 Head
3 Sill
4 Casement sash
5 Awning (vent) sash

Double-hung window
1 Jamb
2 Casing
3 Exterior trim
4 Head
5 Sill
6 Sash
7 Parting stop
8 Sash track
9 Pocket
10 Meeting rail

Pivot window
1 Head
2 Jamb
3 Sill
4 Sash
5 Pivot hardware

Double-hung windows

Vertically sliding windows are usually known as double-hung windows. In this design, both the top and the bottom sash can be opened.

Traditional wooden sash windows (see opposite) are constructed with a box frame in which the jambs are composed of three boards, joined together at the top corners. The side jambs are joined to the sill at the bottom. Windows are sized to fit standard wall thicknesses. When installed, the inside edge of the jambs should be flush with the wall surface and ready for casings to be nailed in place. For thicker walls, extension jambs are nailed to the window jambs to bring them flush with the wall.

If the window has counterweights, they're installed behind the side jambs, with access provided by a small removable piece of the jamb, called a pocket.

The sashes of a double-hung window are held in tracks formed in the side jambs. They are separated by a parting stop. The top sash slides in the outer track and overlaps the bottom sash at horizontal meeting rails. The closing faces of the meeting rails are beveled. This bevel makes the sashes wedge together when closed, which prevents the sashes from rattling. This also allows both rails to separate easily as the window is opened. The sashes are locked by hardware that joins the two when they are in the closed position.

Spiral balances
Modern wooden, aluminum, and vinyl sashes have spring-assisted spiral balances. The balances are attached to the sides of the jambs.

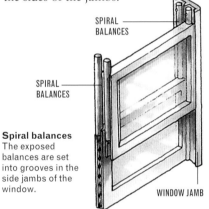

SPIRAL BALANCES

SPIRAL BALANCES

Spiral balances
The exposed balances are set into grooves in the side jambs of the window.

WINDOW JAMB

Aluminum windows
Aluminum window frames are installed in new houses, and often are used as replacement windows for old wood or steel units. The aluminum is extruded into complex sections to hold double-glazed sashes. Finished in several colors—usually white, silver, black, brown, and bronze—aluminum window frames require no maintenance.

They are sold, like wood windows, in many different standard sizes with many different features. They are manufactured in complete units ready for installation. To reduce water damage from condensation, hollow sections of the metal frame incorporate an insulating material to create a thermal break.

Extruded-aluminum window in a wooden frame

Vinyl windows
Rigid vinyl windows are similar to aluminum ones. They are typically manufactured in white plastic and, once installed, require only minimal maintenance.

Extruded-plastic window with metal reinforcing

Pivot windows

Wood-frame pivot windows (see opposite) are constructed in a similar way to casement windows. But their special hinge mechanism allows the sash to be rotated so that both sides of the glass can be cleaned from inside. Using the built-in safety catch, the sash can be locked when open or when fully reversed.

Similar pivoting windows, usually called roof windows, are made for pitched roofs. Thesy are usually double-glazed; some come with built-in blinds. The window is usually protected on the outside by an aluminum cladding, and a flashing kit provides a weatherproof seal between the window and the roof.

Jalousie windows

A jalousie window is a specialized pivot window. The panes are unframed strips of glass, typically ¼ inch thick, that are capped at each end by plastic or aluminum carriers. These carriers pivot on channels screwed to the window frame. The panes are linked by a mechanism that allows them to be opened or closed simultaneously. The exposed edges of the glass are ground and polished.

Jalousie windows provide excellent ventilation and light transmission, but unfortunately offer minimal security unless outfitted with specialized locks.

Use two sets of panes for wide opening.

Frame walls

Most windows today are prefabricated and set in place as a single unit. Installing them is similar to installing prehung doors. First, measure the rough opening to make sure it is large enough to accept the window. Then cover all four sides of the opening with 15-pound roofing felt to reduce water damage if there is a leak. Set the window in the opening from outside. Center it from side to side.

Check the sill for level and the jambs for plumb. On the outside, drive a 10d finishing nail through the exterior casing and into the wall framing. Start a nail in the opposite top corner, check for level and plumb, and drive the nail into the framing.

Measure between diagonal corners to make sure that the window is square (the measurements should be exactly the same) and insert any necessary shims along the sides of the frame to keep it square. Then nail the lower corners. Operate the sashes to make sure they move smoothly, then finish nailing the window in place.

Push insulation between the window frame and the rough framing from the inside. Then install a drip cap above the window. Set all nailheads and fill the holes. Prime and paint the outside of the window.

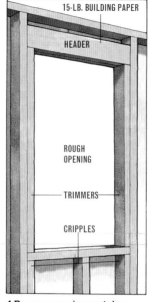

1 Be sure opening matches window
To narrow an opening, install extra trimmers or strips of plywood. To widen an opening, add a new stud next to the framed opening and remove the existing one. Alter the height of an opening by changing the height of the sill, not the header.

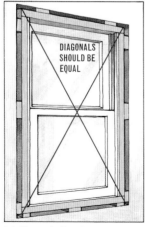

2 Adjust window in opening
Adjust window with shims until it is level, plumb, and square. Make sure the sashes operate smoothly. If diagonals—measured from corner to corner—across the window are equal, the window is square.

3 Nail through casing into studs
Nail window at top corners first, then check for square and nail at bottom corners. Nail every 12 inches between corners. Install drip cap, set nailheads, and fill holes. Caulk around the window.

In older brick houses, it's common to find the windows set into recesses in the walls, instead of being flush with the outside of the walls. The openings were finished first and the windows were made to fit the openings. The windows were nailed or screwed into wood plugs set into the mortar joints. In a typical 9-inch-thick wall, the window was installed so the inside edge of the jambs was even with the interior wall surface.

In traditional brick construction, the bottom of the opening was defined by a stone sill, and the top of the opening was supported by an arch made of brick or with a stone lintel. Wood lintels were installed behind the arches to help support some of the weight.

Stone lintels were sometimes carved with decorative features and they, too, usually had wood lintels behind them to carry some weight. These traditional window openings—at least in residential construction—were never very wide because of the heavy weight above that had to be supported. When a room called for a wide bank of windows, these usually consisted of multiple smaller openings that were divided by brick or stone columns.

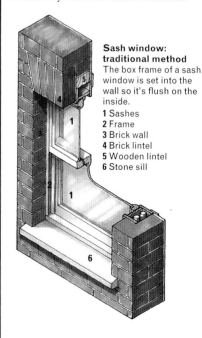

Sash window: traditional method
The box frame of a sash window is set into the wall so it's flush on the inside.
1 Sashes
2 Frame
3 Brick wall
4 Brick lintel
5 Wooden lintel
6 Stone sill

Cutting glass

Always carry panes of glass on edge to prevent them from bending, and wear heavy work gloves to protect your hands. Also wear goggles to protect your eyes when removing broken glass from a frame. Wrap broken glass in thick layers of newspaper before you dispose of it, to reduce the possibility that the people who pick up the trash will be cut. Or check with a local glass shop; it may be willing to add your glass to its scrap pile to be sent back to the manufacturer for recycling.

Basic glass cutting

It is not usually necessary to cut glass at home because most suppliers are willing to do it for you. But sometimes it's more convenient to cut it yourself. A handheld glass cutter with a steel wheel is inexpensive, easy to use, and can handle most common jobs.

Cutting glass successfully is largely a matter of practice and confidence. If you have not done it before, make a few practice cuts on waste pieces of glass and get used to the feel of the tool before cutting the project piece.

Lay the glass on a flat surface covered with a blanket. (Patterned glass should be placed pattern side down and cut on its smooth side.) Clean the cutting surface with mineral spirits.

Place a T-square at the cutline (**1**), and check your measurement. If you're working on a small piece of glass or don't have a T-square, mark the glass on opposing edges with a felt-tipped pen and use a straightedge to join the marks and guide the cutter.

Lubricate the cutter wheel by dipping it in light machine oil or kerosene. Hold the cutter between your middle finger and forefinger (**2**) and draw it along the guide with a single continuous stroke. Use firm, even pressure throughout the stroke and run the cutter off the end. Slide the glass over the edge of the table (**3**) and tap the underside of the scored line with the back of the cutter. Wearing gloves, grip the glass on each side of the scored line (**4**) and snap it in two. Or you can place a wood dowel under the length of the cutline and push down evenly on both sides of the pane until the glass snaps.

1 Measure glass with tape and T-square

2 Cut glass with one continuous stroke

3 Tap underside to initiate cut

4 Snap glass in two

Cutting off a thin strip of glass

To reduce a slightly oversize pane of glass, remove a thin strip by scoring a line as described above, then gradually remove the waste with nibblers (see far left) or a pair of pliers.

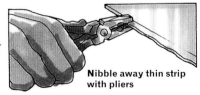
Nibble away thin strip with pliers

You can buy most types of glass from your local hardware store or home center. Often the salespeople can advise you on the type you need and cut the glass to your specifications. If the piece of glass you want is big, or you want to order a lot of glass, look for a glass supply store in the Yellow Pages. Specialty suppliers have a greater selection of different glasses and will usually deliver.

Glass cutters

Glass thickness

Once expressed by weight, the thickness of glass is now measured in inches. If you are replacing old glass, measure its thickness to the nearest $\frac{1}{32}$ of a inch. If you can't find an exact match, buy a slightly thicker glass for safety.

Although there aren't any strict regulations concerning the thickness of glass, it is advisable to comply with the recommendations set out in the Uniform Building Code. The thickness of glass required depends on the area of the pane, its exposure to wind pressure, and the vulnerability of its location, for example, whether it is next to a play area. Tell your supplier what the glass is needed for to ensure that you get the right type.

Glass nibblers
Use nibblers to trim off the edge of a pane.

Measuring

Measure the height and width of the opening to the inside of the frame rabbet. Check each dimension by taking measurements from at least two points. Also check that the diagonals are the same length. If they differ significantly, indicating that the frame is out of square, make a cardboard template of the opening and take it to the glazier. In any case, deduct 1/8 inch from the height and the width to allow room for adjusting the glass when you install it. When ordering an asymmetrical piece of glass, make an exact template of the piece you need and take this to the supplier.

Repairing a broken window

Installing new glass

● **Glazing putty**
Traditional linseed-oil putty is made for glazing wood frames. It dries slowly and is hard when set. All-purpose putty for wood and steel frames has similar properties. Both putties tend to crack if they are not protected with paint. Newer acrylic-based glazing putty is an all-purpose type that is easy to use and dries quickly, ready for painting.

Even when no glass is missing, a cracked windowpane is a safety hazard and a security risk, and no longer provides a weatherproof barrier to the elements. It should be replaced promptly.

Temporary repairs
For temporary protection from the weather, tape a sheet of polyethylene over the outside of the window frame until you can replace the glass. If the window is merely cracked, it can be repaired temporarily using a clear self-adhesive waterproof tape.

Safety with glass
Unless the window is at ground level, it's safer to remove the sash in order to replace broken glass. A fixed window has to be repaired on the spot, wherever it is. Large pieces of glass should be handled by two people. Don't work in windy weather; wear gloves and protective goggles when removing glass.

Buy new glazing points and enough glazing compound for the frame. One pound of putty will fill an average-sized rabbet about 13 feet in length.

Working with putty
Knead a palm-size ball of putty (glazing compound) to an even consistency in your hand. To soften putty that is too stiff, add a little linseed oil. Press a thin, continuous band of putty into the rabbet all around the frame. Smooth it out with a putty knife. Lower the new pane of glass into the bottom rabbet, then press the rest of the pane into place. Apply pressure close to the edges only, squeezing the putty to leave a continuous seal around the whole pane. Secure the glass by installing glazier's points every 8 inches around the

Install new points

pane. Make sure they lay flat with the surface of the glass. Trim the surplus putty from the back of the glass with a putty knife.

Apply more putty to each rabbet on the outside of the glass. Using a putty knife , work the putty to a smooth finish at a 45-degree angle. Make neat miters at the corners. Let the putty set for about three weeks, then paint the frame. The paint should lap the glass slightly to form a weather seal.

Acrylic glazing putty
Acrylic glazing putty is applied with a caulking gun. Run a bead of putty into the rabbet. Bed the glass and secure it with glazing points. Then apply a continuous bead of putty all around the frame and smooth it to a 45-degree angle with a putty knife. Allow at least 4 hours for it to cure, then trim off excess and clean the glass with water.

Repairing glass in wood frames

In wood window frames, the glass is set into a rabbet cut in the frame, and then bedded in putty. Small wedge-shaped fasteners, known as points, are also used to hold the glass in place. Traditionally, linseed-oil putty was used for glazing wood frames. However, acrylic-based glazing putty, which is fast drying and durable, can be used instead. In some cases a wood glass bead is screwed to the rabbet to hold the pane.

Glass held with putty

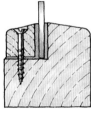

Glass held with bead
Some wood frames feature a wood beading, embedded in putty and screwed to the frame. Unscrew the beading and scrape out the putty. Install new glass in fresh putty and replace the beading.

Removing the glass
If the glass has shattered, leaving jagged pieces set in the putty, grip each piece separately and try to work it loose (**1**). Start working from the top of the frame. Old,dry putty will usually break away easily. But if it won't, cut it out, using a utility knife or a glazier's knife and a

hammer (**2**). Work along the rabbet to remove the putty and glass. Pull out the points with pliers (**3**).

If the glass is merely cracked, run a glass cutter around the perimeter of the pane, about 1 inch from the frame, to score the glass (**4**). Apply strips of tape across the cracks and scored lines, then tap each piece of glass until it breaks free and is held only by the tape (**5**). Carefully remove individual pieces of glass, working from the center of the pane.

Once all the glass and points are removed, clean out all remnants of old putty from the rabbets. Seal the wood with primer. Measure the height and width of the opening to the inside of the rabbets, and have new glass cut ⅛ inch smaller in height and width to provide some room for adjustment.

2 Cut away old putty`

4 Score glass before removing cracked pane

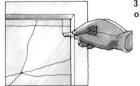

1 Work broken glass loose

3 Pull out old points

5 Tap glass to break it free

The sashes of wood casement windows tend to swell in wet weather, causing them to stick in the frame. Once they dry out, they should work properly and you should take the time to prime and paint them. This will reduce or totally eliminate the swelling because the water won't reach the wood.

Curing sticking windows

If you have a casement window that sticks persistently in all weather, it may be due to a thick buildup of paint. To repair this condition, strip the old paint from the edges of the sash and the rabbets in the frame. Then prime and paint these surfaces.

If a window has been painted shut, free it by working a utility-knife blade between the sash and the frame. Sand the edges smooth until the sash closes properly, remove any dust, then prime and paint the sanded edges. The same repair advice applies to all window sashes that have been painted shut.

Curing rattling windows

The rattling of a casement window is usually caused by a poorly installed lever lock. If the lever handle is worn, you can either replace it with a new one or adjust the position of the old one so it works better.

Old double-hung wood windows are notorious for rattling. The most common cause is a sash (usually the bottom one) that fits too loosely in its tracks. To repair it, remove and replace the stop, or glue a thin strip to the side of the stop, to create a narrower track. Rub candle wax on both sliding surfaces if the repair is a little too tight.

If the top sash is rattling, shim it out in a similar way and adjust the position of the lock to pull the sashes together.

Installing stepped glazing

Some double-glazed window units are designed with a step built into the edge. This provides a positive surface for the unit to bear against. These panes are installed much like regular panels, but a resilient packing piece is added to support the extra weight.

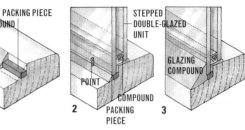

Stepped units
Follow this sequence when installing double-glazed, stepped units.
1 Set the resilient packing in glazing compound.
2 Install the double-glazed unit and secure with glazing points.
3 Fill the rabbet with glazing putty.

Installing square-edged units

Square-edged units are sealed with butyl glazing compound and held in place with beading. For the conventional method shown here, you will need glazing compound, glazing blocks, and beading nails (see below).

Apply two coats of primer or clear sealer to the rabbets in the frame and let them dry. Lay a bed of the nonsetting butyl glazing compound in the rabbets. To prevent the glass from moving in the compound, place packing blocks on the bottom rabbet and place the spacer blocks against the back of the rabbet. Set the spacers about 2 inches from the corners and about 12 inches apart. Locate the spacers directly behind the points where the beading will be screwed in place.

Set the double-glazed unit into the rabbet and press it firmly in place. Apply an outer layer of compound and place another set of spacers against the glass, positioned to match the spacers installed behind the glass.

Press each bead into the compound and against the spacers. Screw the beading strips in place with brass or galvanized screws. Remove the compound that squeezed out and clean the glass. Prime and paint as needed.

Using beading
Set square-edged units in butyl compound.
1 Set the packing and spacers in compound.
2 Install the unit, apply more compound, and place spacers behind the beading screw locations.
3 Press the beading against the spacers and attach with screws.

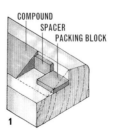
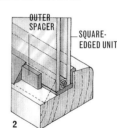
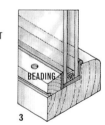

Glazing metal-framed windows

Steel window frames are made with galvanized sections that form a rabbet for the glass. This type of window is glazed in much the same way as a wood-framed window, using general-purpose glazing compound or acrylic glazing putty. The glass is secured with spring clips (see right) set in holes in the frame and covered with putty. To replace the glass in a metal frame, follow the sequence described for wood frames but use clips instead of points. Before installing the glass, remove any rust and apply a high-quality metal primer.

Modern aluminum and plastic double-glazed frames use a dry glazing system that features synthetic rubber gaskets. These are factory installed and should be maintenance free. If you break a pane in a window, consult the manufacturer for the proper way to make the repair.

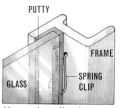

Use spring clips to hold glass

Repairing rotten frames

Replacing a rail in a fixed window

Old wood windows have always deteriorated to some extent. But regular maintenance and prompt repairs can restore them so they work properly for many years to come. New frames and those that have been stripped of their old finish should be treated with a wood preservative before you paint them.

The bottom rail of a wood sash is particularly vulnerable to rot, especially if it is left unpainted. Rainwater seeps in behind old glazing putty, and moisture is gradually absorbed through cracked or flaking paint. Carry out an annual check and deal with any faults. Cut out old putty that has shrunk away from the glass and replace it. Remove flaking paint, repair any cracks in the wood with wood filler, prime, and repaint. Don't forget to paint the bottom edge of the sash.

Replacing a sash rail

Where the rot is so severe that the sash rail is beyond repair, cut it out and replace it. This should be done before the rot spreads to the stiles, otherwise you will eventually have to replace the whole sash frame. Start by removing the sash from the window frame.

It is possible to make the repair without removing the glass, though it is safer to remove it if the window is large. For either approach, you'll need to cut away the putty from the damaged rail.

Usually, the bottom rail is tenoned into the stiles **(1)**. To remove the rail, saw down the joint shoulder lines from both sides of the sash **(2)**.

Make a new sash rail and cut it to length so a full-width tenon is at each end. Position the tenons to line up with the mortises in the stiles. Cut the shoulders of the tenons to match the rabbeted sections of the stiles **(3)**. If there is a decorative molding on the stile, cut it away to leave a flat shoulder **(4)**. Cut slots in the ends of the stiles to receive the new tenons.

Glue the new rail securely into place with a waterproof glue and reinforce the two joints with pairs of ¼-inch hardwood dowels. Drill the stopped holes for the dowels from the inside of the frame so they won't break through the outer surface. Stagger the dowels for a stronger joint.

When the adhesive is dry, plane and sand the surface as needed and remove all the dust. Treat the new wood with a clear preservative. Fill the rail rabbet with glazing compound, then prime and paint as soon as the putty is dry.

The frames of some fixed windows are made like sashes but are screwed permanently to the jamb. After the glass has been removed and the frame unscrewed, this type of fixed window can be repaired in the same way as the casement of sash windows (see below left).

First remove the putty and the glass, then saw through the rail at each end, close to the stile. Use a chisel to remove what remains of the rail and to carve the tenons out of the stiles. Cut a new length of rail to fit between the stiles, and cut slots at both ends of the rail to receive the loose tenons **(1)**. Cut these slots so that they line up with the stile mortises, and make each slot twice as long as the depth of the mortise. Cut two loose tenons to fit the slots, and two packing blocks to force the loose tenons into place. These blocks should have one sloping edge **(2)**.

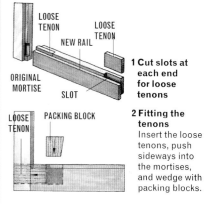

1 Cut slots at each end for loose tenons

2 Fitting the tenons
Insert the loose tenons, push sideways into the mortises, and wedge with packing blocks.

Reassembling the frame

Apply waterproof glue to all joining surfaces. Place the rail between the stiles, insert the loose tenons, and push sideways into the mortises. Drive packing blocks behind the tenons to lock them in. When the adhesive has set, trim the packing blocks flush with the rabbet in the rail. Treat the new wood with preservative, replace the glass, and add new putty. Repaint once the putty is dry.

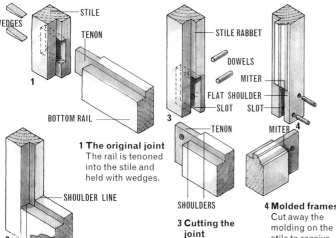

1 The original joint
The rail is tenoned into the stile and held with wedges.

2 Cutting out the rail
Saw down the shoulder lines of the joints from both sides of the sash.

3 Cutting the joint
Cut tenons at each end of the rail, making sure that the shoulders of the joint match the shape of the stile.

4 Molded frames
Cut away the molding on the stile to receive the square shoulder of the rail. Make the cut in the shape of a miter.

Repairing rotten sills

The sill is a fundamental part of a window frame, and because of its size and location, suffers from more exposure to the elements. This exposure can lead to rot. Repairing a sill usually is not a difficult job, but replacing one can be.

A window frame is constructed in much the same way as a doorframe. The head and side jambs are the same width, but the sill is wider and sloped to the outside to shed water. If you just need to repair chips, cracks, and worn depressions, you can work on the sill without removing any window parts. Just choose a day or two when fair weather is forecast. But if you have to replace a wood or stone sill, it's better to remove the window first. If this is impractical, you can replace the sill in place; it's just more difficult.

Replacing a wood sill for a sash window

Ideally, to replace a rotted windowsill you should remove the entire window, carefully disassemble the old sill from the jamb sides, use it as a template, then cut and install a new sill and replace the window. However, sills can be replaced without removing the window, provided you work patiently and have some basic woodworking skills.

Begin by carefully splitting out the old sill. Cut through it crosswise in two places with a saw to remove the middle portion, then gently pry the end sections away from the jambs. Hacksaw any nails holding the sill to the rest of the frame.

Use a piece of cardboard to make a template for a new sill, shaped to fit between the jambs and beneath the exterior trim. Cut a 10-degree bevel along the upper outside edge of the sill, extending to the inside edge of the sash. Fill the area beneath the sill with insulation, install the sill with 16d finishing nails, then thoroughly fill all the seams with silicone caulk.

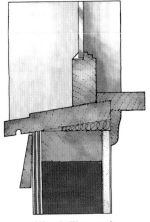

Wood sill on sash window in wood-frame wall

Decaying windowsills
Repair deteriorating sills before serious decay sets in.

Repairing a stone subsill

The traditional stone sills featured in older houses may become eroded by the weather if they are not protected with paint. They may also suffer cracking due to subsidence in some part of the wall.

Repair any cracked and eroded surfaces with a quick-setting waterproof cement. To do this, clean any dust or debris from the cracks. Then dampen the stone with clean water and work the cement well into the cracks. Smooth the surface of the patch flush with the surface of the sill.

Depressions caused by erosion should be undercut to provide the cement with a good hold. A thin layer of cement simply applied to a shallow depression in the surface will not last. Use a cold chisel to cut away the surface of the sill at least 1 inch below the finished level and remove all traces of dust.

Make a wooden form to the shape of the sill and temporarily nail it to the wall. Dampen the stone, pour in the cement until it's level with the top of the form, then smooth it with a trowel. Allow the patch to cure for a couple of days before removing the form.

Encase sill in wood form to make repair

Casting a new subsill

Cut out the remains of the old stone sill with a hammer and cold chisel. Make a wood form shaped exactly like the old sill. The form must be made upside down, its open top representing the underside of the sill. Fill two-thirds of the mold with fine aggregate concrete, tamped down well. Then add two lengths of steel reinforcing bar (rebar), in the middle of the concrete, and fill the remainder of the form. Set a piece of ⅜ inch wood dowel into notches previously cut in the ends of the mold. This is to form a drip groove in the underside of the sill.

Cover the concrete with polyethylene sheeting or dampen it regularly for two or three days to prevent rapid drying. When the concrete is set (allow about seven days), remove it from the form and clean up any rough edges with a cold chisel or handheld power grinder. Reinstall the sill in a bed of mortar, and caulk all joints with silicone caulk.

REINFORCING BARS

DOWEL

SILL FORM

SHAPED TO MATCH SILL

Replacing broken sash cords

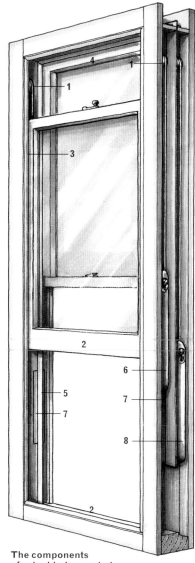

**The components
of a double-hung window**

1 Pulleys   5 Parting stop
2 Bottom sash   6 Bottom sash
3 Exterior trim   weight
4 Top sash   7 Pocket
          8 Top sash
            weight

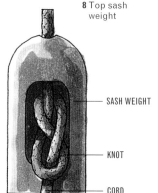

Sash weight knot

The cords that support sashes in most older windows wear out over time and must be replaced for the window to operate properly. When replacing these cords, always do both sides of the window, even if only one cord is broken. The cords are usually sold by the foot. Each sash requires two lengths about three-quarters the height of the window. Narrow sash chain is also available, and most people consider it more durable than cord.

Removing the sashes

Lower the sashes and cut through the cords with a utility knife to release the weights. Hold on to the cords and lower the weights as far as possible before letting them drop. Using a screwdriver, pry off the side access panels from the sash tracks so the weight pockets will be exposed.

Lean the inner sash forward and mark the ends of the cord grooves on the face of the sash stiles (**1,** see below). Reposition the sash and transfer the marks onto the window jambs. The sash can now be pulled clear of the frame.

Carefully pry out the two parting stops from their grooves in the jambs. You can use a flat-blade screwdriver or a chisel to do this job. Start at one end, prying gradually as you go. If a stop won't budge, grip it with pliers and pull as you pry with the screwdriver.

Once the stops are out, and you've marked the end-cord grooves as before, remove the top sash and place it safely aside. Then remove the window weights from the pockets by pulling them through the access holes. Cut the old cord from the weights and sashes and clean up the weights so they're ready for the new sash cords.

Reinstalling the sashes

The top sash is installed first, but not before all of the sash cords and weights are in place. Clean away any buildup of paint from the pulleys. Tie a length of fine string to one end of the sash cord. Weight the other end of the string with small nuts or a piece of chain. Thread the weight over a pulley (**2**) and pull the string through the pocket opening until the cord is pulled through. Attach the end of the cord to a weight with a special knot (see below left).

Use the sash marks to measure the length of cord required. Pull on the cord to hoist the weight up to the pulley. Then let it drop back about 4 inches. Hold it temporarily in this position with a nail driven into the window jamb just below the pulley. Cut the cord even with the mark on the pulley jamb (**3**). Repeat this procedure for the cord on the other side of the upper sash and do the

same for the bottom sash.

Lift the top sash into its track and remove the nail that holds one of the sash cords. Lean the sash forward, push the cord into its groove in the sash stile, and nail it in place using three or four 1-inch nails. Nail only the bottom 6 inches, not all the way up (**4**).

Do the same thing for the other sash cord, then lift the sash to check that the weights work properly and do not touch the bottom. Replace the pocket-access door and the parting stop. Then install the bottom sash and attach it to the cords the same way.

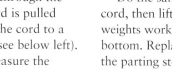

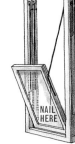

1 Mark cord grooves   2 Pull cord through   3 Cut cords at mark   4 Nail cord to sash

Spiral balances

Instead of cords and counterweights, modern sash windows use spiral balances that are mounted on the inside of the window jambs, eliminating the need for traditional weight boxes. The balances are made to match the size and weight of individual glazed sashes and can be ordered from the window manufacturers at your local lumberyard or home center.

Spiral balance components
Each balance consists of a torsion spring and a spiral rod housed in a tube. The top end is fixed to the jamb and the inner spiral is attached to the bottom of the sash. The complete unit is housed in a sash or jamb groove.

Installing the balances

One of the great things about spiral balances is that you can use them to replace window weights in older sash windows. To do this, first remove the sashes and weigh them on your bathroom scale. Place your order, giving the weight of each sash, its height and width, and the overall inside height of the window frame. Reinstall the sashes until the balances arrive, then take the sashes out again and remove the pulleys.

Plug the holes in the sashes with wood filler. Cut grooves, as specified by the manufacturer, in the stiles of each sash to take the balances (1). Cut a mortise at each end of the bottom edges of the stiles to receive the spiral-rod mounting plates. Install the plates with screws (2).

Push the top sash in place, resting it on the sill. Take the top pair of balances, which are shorter than those for the bottom sash, and install each in its groove (3). Attach the top ends of the balance tubes to the frame jambs (4), pushing the ends tight against the top jamb.

Lift the sash to its full height and prop it with a scrap of wood. Hook the wire "key," provided with the balances, into the hole in the end of each spiral rod. Adjust the tension on the spiral spring according to the maker's instructions (5). Attach the end of each rod to its mounting plate and test the balance of the sash. If it drops, add another turn on the springs until it is just held in position. Take care not to overwind the balances.

Install the bottom sash and balances in the same way. Once you're satisfied with the operation of both sashes, install the stops that limit the full travel of the sashes in their respective tracks (see far left).

● **Renovating spiral balances**
In time, the springs of spiral balances may weaken. To retension them , unhook the spiral rods from the mounting plates, then turn the rods counterclockwise once or twice.
 To service the mechanism, release the tension and unwind the rods from the tubes. Wipe them clean and apply a coat of light oil, then rewind the rods back into the tubes and tension them as described above.

Sash window with balances
1 Top limit stop
2 Top sash balance
3 Bottom sash balance
4 Mounting plate
5 Mounting plate
6 Bottom limit stop
7 Top sash
8 Bottom sash

TUBE

SPIRAL

PLATE

Spiral balance unit

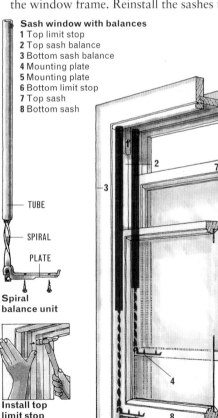

Install top limit stop

Install bottom stop

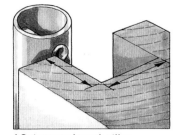

1 Cut groove in sash stiles

2 Secure mounting plate with screws

3 Install sash and insert tube in its groove

4 Nail top end of tube to jamb

5 Tension springs with the provided key

Lumberyards and home centers offer a wide range of replacement windows in wood, vinyl, and aluminum. Some typical examples are shown below.

Unfortunately, the exact window size you need may not be available. You have two options: Order custom-made windows to fit your openings or modify your rough openings to fit a standard replacement-window size.

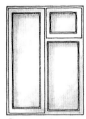

Casement window

Most people replace their windows either because they don't work well mechanically, or because they allow too much heat to escape in the winter.

Replacing windows is an expensive job, so it's tempting to use low-cost units. Unfortunately, these windows don't always solve the problems you're having. The long-term performance and energy savings of higher-quality windows are usually worth the extra cost.

Vertical sliding sash window

The style of the windows is an important element in the appearance of any house. If you are thinking of replacing the windows in an older house you might find it better, and not necessarily more expensive, to have new windows custom made to fit your openings.

Planning and permits

Window replacement is a job that doesn't usually require a building permit, unless you live in a historic district that regulates what you can do to the exterior of your house. But if you plan to alter your windows significantly—for example, by permanently removing one or by adding a new window in a new place— you should call your local building department to see if you need a permit.

All codes have certain minimum requirements, especially for windows on second and third floors. Code authorities want to make sure that at least some windows are big enough for occupants to get out in case of fire. Some localities are also interested in the R-value of the window glazing, in an effort to improve the energy efficiency of the housing stock.

Buying replacement windows

As mentioned earlier, replacing windows can be a problem if your window openings do not match the standard sizes available from most window manufacturers. You'll either have to alter your openings to fit standard sizes (which can be nearly as expensive as buying the new windows), or you can buy custom-made windows that will fit your openings.

Usually the term custom made is used for one-of-a-kind items that tend to be very expensive. But several large manufacturers will make just about any size window for a relatively small additional charge. Unfortunately, the manufacturers who offer this service are making windows that are expensive in the first place.

Most contractors who install replacement windows supply the new windows and dispose of the old ones after removal. This is the best way to get the job done, but you should carefully compare contractors and window brands before making your choice.

Replacing casements

Measure the width and height of the window opening. Windows in brick walls will need a wood subframe. If the existing one is in good condition, take your measurements from the inside of this frame. Otherwise, take them from the brick and plan on replacing the frame before installing the new window. Order the replacement window accordingly.

Remove the old window by first taking out the sashes. Remove any exposed hardware that may be holding the window frame in the opening. Pry out the frame and cut through any fasteners with a hacksaw or a reciprocating saw. Usually the frame can be pried or driven out of the opening in

one piece. But if it's wedged tight for some reason, saw through it in several places and pry the pieces out with a crowbar **(1)**. Clean up the opening.

Remove all the protective packaging from the window and slide it into the opening. Check it for level and plumb **(2)** and shim the jambs to keep the unit from moving. Drill screw holes through the jambs into the jack studs or the subframe behind the window jambs **(3)**. Check for level and plumb again, then drive the screws.

Insulate around the window frame, then install any necessary exterior trim and the interior casings. Set all nailheads and cover them with wood filler or caulk. Prime and paint.

1 Pry out pieces of old frame

2 Install new window

3 Drill screw holes

Bay windows

A bay window is an assembly of smaller windows joined together to yield a big window that projects out from the house wall. The side windows are usually set at one of three angles: 90, 60, or 45 degrees. Curved bays are also available.

The perimeter of a bay window is supported either with brackets of different types or with a shout wall that is part of the wall framing. The bay is protected by a small roof that is attached to the house wall.

Bay windows in brick houses can break away from the main wall because of foundation subsidence. You should hire a contractor for this type of problem. Lesser damage from slight foundation movements can be repaired once the ground has stabilized. Repoint the mortar joints and apply silicone caulk to gaps around the window frame.

Replacement bays

Like other windows, old bay windows can be replaced with new ones. But your chances of finding a new bay in just the right size are slight. Usually the opening has to be adjusted, which for bays is complicated by the presence of the roof. Choosing a custom-made bay is probably your best strategy. It may be more expensive, but using something the right size should keep the installation costs to a minimum.

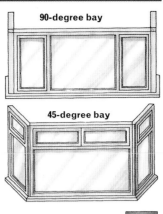
90-degree bay

45-degree bay

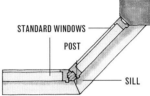
STANDARD WINDOWS

POST

SILL

Modern angled bay with decorative lead flashing

Standard windows joined to make a bay window

Bow windows

These are windows constructed on a shallow curve, and (like bay windows) they normally project from a flat wall. Complete bow windows are available from window manufacturers, ready for installation. You can use a bow window to replace any type of window, as long as the rough opening is big enough to fit the new window.

To installs a bow window, modify the rough opening as necessary. Then center the bow in the opening, shim it plumb and level, then nail it into place. Install braces beneath the window to support it. And construct a shallow roof over the top to shed rain and snow. Add flashing and new trim where necessary, then caulk all the joints with silicone caulk. Add insulation between the window and the rough opening, then install the interior trim.

First-floor bow window

Window replacement in a brick wall isn't much more difficult than replacing a window in a wood-frame wall. The job is well within the ability of most do-it-yourselfers.

Remove the sashes, then take out the old window frame from inside the room. Pry off the casing, then the window jamb. Cut away the drywall or plaster if necessary. Remove any obvious fasteners holding the frame to the brick, then strike the outside edge of the sill with a heavy hammer and a wood block. When the window frame is free, lift it out of the opening (1) and remove any debris left behind.

Lift the new window into the opening and adjust it from front to back so that both side jambs are the same distance from the outside of the brick wall. Check the window frame for level and plumb and wedge the corners of the frame at the top and the sill. If there's space left at the sides between the window and the brick wall, fill the space with bricks and mortar (2). To solidly anchor the window, you can screw metal brackets to the sides of the window frame and set these brackets in mortar joints in the brick wall.

When the mortar is set, replaster the inner wall and replace the casing. Finish up by applying silicone caulk to the joints between the outside bricks and the window frame to keep the weather out.

1 Lift out old frame   **2 Fill gaps with brick**

Roof windows

Roof windows used in a traditional building

Double-glazed roof windows are becoming increasingly popular for replacing old skylights, especially on attic-conversion jobs. The windows usually come with complete flashing kits that are designed to fit a wide range of different roof pitches.

Roof windows that have center-pivoting sashes can be used on just about all roofs. Because the sash in these windows operates, the window can provide ventilation as well as lots of light. They are relatively easy to install using only common remodeling tools. And most of the work is done from inside the house. Once they are installed, the glass can be cleaned comfortably from the inside. Accessories like built-in blinds and remote-opening devices are also available. Most manufacturers also give you glazing options to reduce heat loss and sun glare.

Window height
The height should enable someone sitting or standing to see out of the window with ease.

Choosing the size

The manufacturers of roof windows offer a wide range of standard sizes. Apart from cost considerations, the overall size of the window should be based on the amount of daylight you want in the room.

The installed height of the window is also important. It should be determined by the pitch of the roof and by how the window is going to be used. Manufacturers produce charts that give the recommended dimensions depending on the roof pitch. Ideally, if the window is to provide a good view, the bottom rails should not obstruct that view at normal seating height. And the top of the window shouldn't cut across the line of sight of someone who is standing.

Generally, this means that the shallower the pitch of the roof, the taller the window needs to be. The top of the window should remain within comfortable reach for accessibility.

Smaller window units can be arranged side by side or one above the other to create a larger window. When deciding on a design, bear in mind how it will look on the outside of the house, not just on the inside.

Though you probably won't need permission to install the window if you're replacing an old unit, code restrictions often apply to any job that requires cutting a new hole through the roof. Check with your building department before beginning work.

The manufacturers of roof windows supply instructions for all types of roofs. Below is a summary of how to install a roof window in an ordinary asphalt shingle roof.

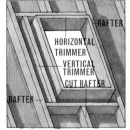

Cut opening and fit trimmers

Installing a roof window

Start by stripping off the roof-covering materials over the area to be occupied by the window. The final placing of the frame will be determined by the position of the rafters and the roofing. Start by setting the bottom of the window frame at the specified distance above the nearest full course of shingles and try to position it so you'll have half or whole shingles at the sides.

Brace the rafters from inside by installing posts beneath them. Then cut through the roof sheathing and rafters to make the opening, following the dimensions given by the manufacturer. Cut and nail headers and trimmers to the opening (see left) to achieve the correct height and width.

With the glazed sash removed, screw the window frame in place with the brackets provided. Make sure the top of the frame is level, and check that the frame is square by measuring across its diagonals; they should be equal.

Complete the outside work by installing the flashing and new shingles, working up from the bottom of the frame. Replace the sash.

Install insulation between the window frame and the rough opening and replace the insulation in other accessible areas if it was damaged during construction. Install drywall panels to close up the opening around the window and finish all the drywall joints with compound and tape. Add trim to the inside of the window jambs and prime and paint the ceiling.

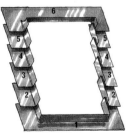

Flashing kit showing order of assembly

Installing curtain rails and rods

Window treatments play an important part in interior design. Although the size and shape of the window itself cannot be altered easily, you can visually modify the proportions of a window with curtains or blinds.

Curtain rails

As well as providing privacy, curtains help insulate the room from the sun, cold, drafts, and noise. They are sold in a variety of fabrics and sizes, or you can make your own. Both the choice of material and the method used for hanging the curtains make an impact.

Modern curtain rods are made from plastic, aluminum, or painted steel. They are available in various styles and lengths and come complete with brackets and rings or hooks. Some are supplied with cords to make drawing the curtains easier and to minimize stains that result from handling.

Although typically used in straight lengths, most rods can be bent to fit a bay window. Rails vary in rigidity, which dictates the minimum radius to which they can be bent.

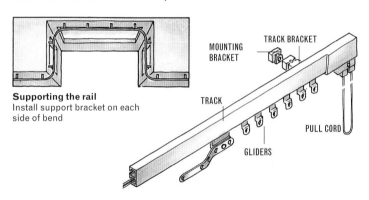

Supporting the rail
Install support bracket on each side of bend

TRACK BRACKET
MOUNTING BRACKET
TRACK
PULL CORD
GLIDERS

Curtain rods

Traditional curtain rods are a popular alternative to modern track systems. Made from metal, plastic, or wood, curtain rods come in a range of plated, painted, or polished finishes. Traditional rods are supported on decoratively shaped brackets and are fitted with end-stop finials and large curtain rings. Some modern versions conceal corded tracks, providing the convenience of up-to-date mechanisms while retaining a traditional look.

A pair of wall brackets are all that's normally required to support curtain rods. But a central bracket may be required to support heavy fabrics. Like the rods, the support brackets are available in many different designs and finishes.

Attaching to the ceiling

Joists that run at right angles to the wall allow you to place curtain track rails at any convenient distance from the wall **(1)**. Drill pilot holes into the joists and screw the brackets in place.

Joists that run parallel to the wall need blocking nailed between them for the tracks **(2)**. Toenail the blocking flush with the ceiling.

If the required track position is close to a joist, nail a 2 x 2 cleat to the face of the joist **(3)**.

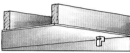

1 Screw to joists

2 Nail blocking in place

3 Nail a cleat in place

Attaching to the wall

Draw a guideline at a suitable height above the window. Mark the positions for the brackets along this line. If you have a wood-frame wall, the brackets must be screwed into framing members behind the wall finish. If you're working on a masonry wall, drill holes for expanding anchors and slide the anchors into place. Then attach the brackets with screws driven into the anchors.

In many cases, you'll be able to mount the brackets on the head casing at the top of the window, especially if you're installing lightweight curtains.

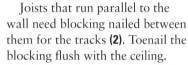

TWO-PIECE WALLBRACKETS
FINIAL
RINGS
POLE
EXTENSION ARM
TRACK BRACKET
MOUNTING BRACKET
ROD TRACK
PULL CORD
RING GLIDERS

Hanging shades and blinds

Blinds provide a simple, attractive, and sophisticated way to screen windows. Most blinds are sold in standard sizes that you can cut easily to the exact length you need. You can also order blinds made to size in many different materials and colors and with different opening and closing mechanisms.

Roller shades

Low-cost roller shades can be bought in a range of fabric designs and colors either made-to-order or in kit form. A typical kit consists of a roller with two end caps (one of which includes a pull-cord mechanism), two support brackets, a thin piece of wood, and a pull cord. You can buy the fabric

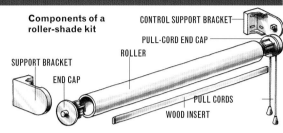

Components of a roller-shade kit

CONTROL SUPPORT BRACKET
PULL-CORD END CAP
ROLLER
SUPPORT BRACKET
END CAP
PULL CORDS
WOOD INSERT

separately and cut it to width and length. The rollers come in several lengths. Unless you can find a roller that fits your window exactly, get the next largest size and cut it to fit.

Cutting to size
A shade can be hung within the window recess or across the front of it. When installing the roller inside, place the brackets in the top corners of the frame. Make sure that the pull-cord control bracket is at the end where you want to operate the shade. Measure and cut the roller to fit between the brackets.

If you are installing the roller outside the window recess, you will need to cut the roller about 4 inches longer than the width of the opening. Install the brackets on both sides of the window, using the roller as a guide.

Fitting the fabric
Ideally the fabric should be nonfraying to avoid having to sew side hems. Cut the width ⅛ inch less than the length of the roller. The fabric length should match the height of the window, plus 8 inches. Make a ¼-inch

bottom hem, then turn it up to form a sleeve for the wood insert. Attach the other end of the fabric to the roller with glue or tape. Make sure the fabric is installed squarely on the roller or the shade won't roll up properly.

Installing the shade
With the fabric rolled on the roller, push the square hole of the pull-cord end cap into the control bracket, with the cords hanging down. Clip the other end into the opposite bracket. Identify the cord that lowers the shade, attach a knob on the end of it, then pull down the cord until it's level with the sill.

Remove the shade and unwind the fabric till it reaches the sill. Reinstall the blind and raise it to the open position, using the other cord, then attach its knob. Check that the blind operates smoothly and, if necessary, adjust the length of the cords.

Vertical blinds

Like horizontal blinds, vertical blinds suit simple modern interiors and work well with large glass openings like patio doors. The blinds hang from a track that is mounted to the ceiling or to the wall above the window or door. The vertical "vanes" that clip into hooks on the track are linked together by short chains at the bottom. The vanes are weighted so that they hang straight.

Installing the track
Mark a guideline on the wall or ceiling. Allow sufficient clearance for the rotating vanes to clear obstacles such as door handles. Screw the mounting brackets in place and clip the track into them. Hang the preassembled vanes on the track hooks. Make sure that the hooks are facing the same way and that you are attaching the vanes with their seams all in the same direction.

Venetian blinds

Horizontal blinds, or Venetian blinds, as they are often called, are popular and stylish window treatments. They come in a range of standard sizes and can be made to order. They are usually fabricated of metal or plastic and are available in many different colors and finishes. A wide variety of wood-slat blinds is also available.

Installing a Venetian blind
If the blind is to be fitted into a window recess, measure the width at the top and bottom of the opening. If the dimensions differ, use the smaller one. Allow a clearance of about ⅛ inch at both ends. Screw the brackets in place so that the blind, when hanging, will clear any handles or catches. Attach the end brackets about 3 inches in from the ends of the head rail.

Mount the head rail in the brackets. Some are simply clamped, while others are locked in place by a swivel catch (**1**). Raise and lower the blind to check that the mechanism is working freely. To lower the blind, pull the cord across the front of the blind to release the lock mechanism, then let it slide through your hand. Tilt the slats by rotating the control wand.

1 Install head rail on bracket.

2 Attach bottom of blind cords to mounting bracket.

Installing at an angle
Venetian blinds can be used on a sloping window. They are supplied with cords that prevent the blind from sagging. When threaded through the slat holes, both cords are attached to the head rail and are held taut by mounting brackets at the bottom (**2**).

Interior shutters

Louvered wooden shutters provide an attractive and practical alternative to fabric curtains or blinds, adding a touch of style to just about any interior. Made from a variety of solid woods, they can be varnished to retain their natural appearance or stained or painted to complement any scheme.

Adjustable-louver shutters

Adjustable-louver shutters are usually sold in standard sizes that are cut to fit specific windows. Made-to-order versions are available, though they're usually quite expensive. The adjustable slats are connected by a slim, vertical wood bar that enables the entire bank of louvers to be set at the same angle. This action controls the amount of natural light passing through the window. When shutters are fully closed, they provide complete privacy.

Shutter combinations

The arrangement of shutters is largely determined by the size of the window opening. A single row of shutters (between two and four panels of uniform width) is a common combination. Two pairs of hinged panels, forming bifold shutters, are perhaps the most popular **(1)**. Where the shutters exceed about 44 inches in height, they are made with a cross rail in the middle to stiffen the frame.

Two or three shorter rows can be stacked one above the other in order to cover tall windows **(2)**. With this arrangement, you can keep one or more rows closed while folding back the remaining row to illuminate the room. When planning for stacked shutters, try to arrange the horizontal divisions between the shutters to align with the cross rails of the window frame. This often looks the best. Or, if you prefer, keep all the panels the same size.

A single row of shutters that cover only half the window are sometimes called café-style shutters **(3)**. They provide some privacy but less control over the level of illumination.

1 Single row shutters

2 Stacked shutters

3 Café-style shutters

Mounting the shutters

Usually, shutters are supplied hinged to a mounting board for screwing to the wall or window frame. You can mount this board on the face of the wall so they span the window opening **(1)**. Or, if you have a deep window, you may want to install the board to the inside of the recess **(2)** or to the sides of the window frame **(3)**. Large shutters, like those used for French windows, for example, can be hung from the top on a bifold-door track system.

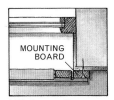

MOUNTING BOARD

1 Wall mounting

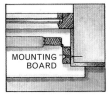

MOUNTING BOARD

2 Recess mounting

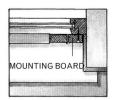

MOUNTING BOARD

3 Window-frame mounting

Face mounting

For shutters to be attached to the face of a wall (see bottom left), measure the height (from the sill) and the width of the window opening. Make an allowance for the shutters to overlap the wall at the top and sides of the opening. And check that the mounting screws won't be too close to the edges of the opening.

Recess mounting

For shutters that are to be mounted in a window recess, measure the width of the opening at the top and bottom. Measure the height at both sides. Use the smaller dimension in both cases. Also, be sure to allow for the thickness of the mounting board at both sides. Check this with your supplier for the size of these boards on the shutters you want to buy.

To determine the size of individual shutters, divide the measured area by the number of shutters you want for each window.

Finishing shutters

Shutters are generally sold fine-sanded for finishing but can be supplied ready finished, if required. You can use a brush to apply a clear finish, colored paint, or wood dye—but covering the numerous faces and edges is time consuming, and it's difficult to avoid leaving runs. Consequently, it's preferable to spray a finish onto shutters. You can hire professional spray equipment, though for just one or two shutters, you will probably be able to make do with pressurized spray cans.

Apply a primer to the bare wood, then rub it down and apply one or two coats of finish. For a stained finish—which will allow the grain of the wood to show—apply one or two even coats of wood dye.

Shelving can be anything from particleboard planks on simple metal brackets to elegant spans of polished hardwood covering an entire library wall. Shelving is generally the simplest, quickest, and most economical form of storage you can find. And if you opt for one of the many adjustable systems, you can adapt your shelving to suit different needs in the future.

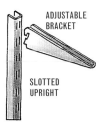

Stamped steel shelf brackets

ADJUSTABLE BRACKET

SLOTTED UPRIGHT

Adjustable-bracket systems

Wall-hung shelves

Shelves can be attached directly to the wall with support boards and end uprights or cantilevered off a wall with any one of a wide range of shelving brackets. These brackets are made of different metals and can support an enormous amount of weight.

Adjustable shelving systems have brackets that clip into upright metal supports screwed to the wall studs. Most uprights have holes or slots at very close intervals so you can make fine adjustments to shelf heights.

One advantage of these systems is that the weight and stress of the loaded shelves are distributed directly to the wall framing, and thus the whole structure of the house. Once the uprights are in place, the shelving arrangements can be changed easily without changing the impact on the support system.

Use inexpensive steel tracks and brackets (with plywood shelves) for utilitarian purposes, such as in your garage or basement. Choose more attractive brackets and shelving for your storage needs around the house.

The simplest way to make built-in, open shelves is to install them in wall recesses, like the alcoves that often flank a fireplace. These areas aren't always plumb and square, so careful fitting of the shelves is usually required to get professional results.

Installing fixed shelves

Mark the position of each shelf, making sure that the spaces between will accommodate all the items you want to store. Using a long level as a guide, draw a level line from each mark across the wall.

Cut wood support cleats for the ends of the shelves. (If the shelves are more than 4 feet long, you should install a cleat across the wall to support the back of the shelf.) For simple shelves, cut the front ends of the cleats to a 45-degree angle **(1)**. For a better appearance, apply wood edging to the front edges of the shelves **(2)**. These make the shelving look more substantial and hide the cleats. For a sleeker appearance, use painted angle iron for your cleats **(3)**.

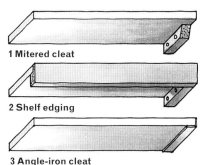

1 Mitered cleat

2 Shelf edging

3 Angle-iron cleat

Precut shelves made from solid wood or manufactured panels are available from lumberyards and home centers in a range of standard sizes. The panels are usually prepainted or covered with wood veneer. Shelves manufactured from glass or painted stamped steel are also widely available. If these kinds of standard shelving don't meet your needs, make your own, using any of the materials shown here.

Materials for shelving

Solid wood
Softwoods, usually pine, hemlock, or fir, are a good choice for shelving, especially if you plan to paint the shelves. Painting covers up the knots that these boards usually have. Softwoods are easy to work with, relatively inexpensive, and available at lumberyards and home centers.

Hardwoods, such as oak, maple, ash, and mahogany are available from hardwood suppliers. These woods are beautiful, but they are harder to work with and almost always more expensive.

Lumber-core plywood
Lumber-core plywood is a relatively expensive manufactured panel made from blocks of softwood glued and sandwiched between two layers of wood veneer. These panels are as strong as solid wood and much more stable. Their exposed edges must be trimmed with veneer or solid wood edging.

Standard plywood
Plywood is built up from veneers, with the grain alternating at right angles in order to provide strength and stability. The exposed edges must be covered with a solid wood edging or veneer.

Particleboard
The least-expensive manufactured panel, particleboard is a popular choice for all types of utility shelving, typically used in basements, garages, and attics.

Medium-density fiberboard
Medium-density fiberboard (MDF) is a dense, stable, man-made panel that is easy to cut and machine. It has a uniform appearance throughout the board, so the edges don't need to be covered with wood or veneer. MDF is ideal for painting.

Glass
Glass is an attractive material for all kinds of shelving. Choose tempered glass and have it cut to size and the edges ground smooth and polished by the supplier.

Stop your shelves from sagging

Solid wood and lumber-core plywood, with its core running lengthways, are the best choices for sturdy shelving. But a shelf made from either material will sag if its supports are too far apart. Particleboard, though popular because of its low cost and availability, will eventually sag under relatively light loads, so it needs supporting at closer intervals than solid wood.

The chart below shows recommended maximum spans for shelves made from different materials. Display shelving for photos and collectibles is generally considered to be under a light load. A shelf full of books is a heavy load. If you want to increase the length of the shelf, then move the supports closer together, add another bracket, or use thicker material for the shelf.

RECOMMENDED SHELF SPANS				
Material	**Thickness**	**Light load**	**Medium load**	**Heavy load**
Solid wood	¾ inch	2 feet 8 inches	2 feet 6 inches	2 feet 4 inches
Lumber-core ply.	¾ inch	2 feet 8 inches	2 feet 6 inches	2 feet 4 inches
Particleboard	⅝ inch	2 feet 6 inches	2 feet	1 feet 6 inches
MDF	¾ inch	2 feet 8 inches	2 feet 6 inches	2 feet 4 inches
Glass	¼ inch	2 feet 4 inches	Not applicable	Not applicable

Stiffening your shelves

A wood edging strip or a metal angle attached to or underneath the front edge of a shelf will increase its stiffness. Where needed, a wall-mounted cleat should be used to support the back edge. A front rail can be used to conceal a thin fluorescent light fixture.

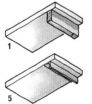
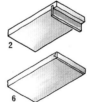
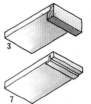
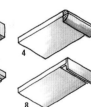

Wood stiffeners
1 Wood rail
2 Plywood strip
3 Rabbeted edging
4 Half-round edging

Metal stiffeners
5 Attached angle
6 Grooved T-section
7 Grooved angle
8 Attached T-section

To a large extent, the nature of your walls will determine the way in which you hang the shelves. On a masonry wall, for example, you can attach the shelf supports almost anywhere, using expansion anchors. On a wood-framed wall, the mounting screws should be driven through the wall finish and into the studs.

Loads cantilevered from wall brackets impose a lot of stress on the installation screws, especially the top ones. If the screws are too small they can be pulled out of the wall by the weight on the shelves.

Shelf supports for wood-frame walls are supplied with the proper screws for the job. If the shelves will be supporting an abnormally heavy load, just use bigger screws.

For ordinary shelving attached to a masonry wall, expansion anchors with 2-inch screws should be adequate. Wide shelves that are to bear a heavy load may well need heavier anchors and screws. Installing extra brackets to prevent the shelf from sagging will help spread the weight. The brackets should be nearly as long as the shelf is wide for the best support.

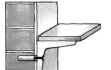

Masonry wall
Use anchors to secure brackets.

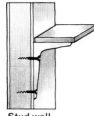

Stud wall
Screw brackets into the wall studs.

Installing individual shelf brackets

To install individual shelf brackets on a wood-frame wall, first locate the studs inside the wall. Studs are usually on 16-inch centers, so once you find one you can quickly locate the others. Mark the wall at the stud locations, then draw a level line across the wall at the desired shelf height. Install brackets where the level and stud lines intersect. Drill pilot holes for the screws, then hang the brackets.

On masonry walls, start by drawing a level line across the wall at shelf height. Then establish the bracket locations on the wall. You can install a bracket anywhere along the line because masonry walls are solid.

Mark the bracket-mounting holes on the walls and drill clearance holes into the wall. Slide the anchors in the holes, hold the bracket in place, and drive the mounting screws into the anchors.

Cut the shelving to size and attach each board to the brackets with screws.

Installing a shelving system

1 Plumb the upright support
Use a level to plumb the upright, then mark the bottom screw hole on the wall.

2 Shimming out the upright support
Push wood shims behind the upright until it is plumb.

The upright supports must be installed plumb. One good way to do this is to loosely attach each upright to the wall with its top screw. Then, hold a level against the upright and adjust it until it's plumb. Mark the position of the bottom screw (1) and install it. Next, check that the upright is plumb in the other direction—does it lean into or away from the room? If it's out of plumb, shim behind the upright to correct it (2).

Install a shelf bracket in the first upright and install another bracket in the next upright. Hold the second upright against the wall and get someone to help you lay a shelf across the brackets. Using a level, check to see if the shelf is level from side to side. If it is, mark the top hole of the second upright and attach it to the wall as you did the first.

Continue in this manner until all the uprights, brackets, and shelves have been installed.

Stairs

Stairs are a series of steps that link one floor with another. But a staircase—the stairs and the walls and trim surrounding them—can also be a powerful expression of the style of the house itself. Because of its location, scale, and shape or decorative features, the staircase is one of the most dominant design elements in a home's interior.

Steps

Each step of an ordinary straight flight of stairs is made from two boards—the vertical riser that forms the front of the step and the horizontal tread, the board on which you walk. The riser is a stiffening member and is installed between two treads, giving support to the front edge of one and the rear of the other. Treads and risers may be joined together in a number of ways. They can also be joined to the stair stringers on the sides in different ways.

Open-tread stairs have thick treads and no risers. They are often used for utility stairs in basements and attics. For increased strength, metal tie rods are sometimes installed across the stairs where the risers would normally be located.

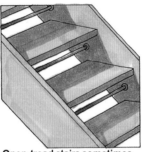

Most staircases have treads and risers

Open-tread stairs sometimes have tie rods

Stringers

Steps are supported at their ends by wide boards set on edge, known as stringers. These are the main structural members that run from one floor level to another. A wall stringer is the inner one which is fixed to the wall. The stringer on the open side of the stair is called the outer stringer. The appearance of the stairs is affected by the style of the stringers. There are two basic types. A closed stringer covers the ends of the stairs, while an open stringer is cut away for each stair, and the stair tread sits on top of the stringer. The closed version is used for the wall stringer and generally matches the height of the baseboard. The outer stringer can be either the closed or the open type.

A closed stringer covers stair ends

An open stringer is cut to the shape of stairs

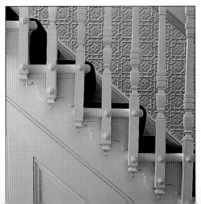

Types of staircases

The simplest staircase, and the one that usually takes up the most room, is a straight flight of steps. Where space is limited, shorter flights may be used, with an intermediate landing linking one flight with another.

Staircase with a half-landing

Most staircases have straight treads, but some have tapered treads, often called winders, that are used to make tight turns.

Winders may be used exclusively to form a sweeping, curved staircase. A spiral staircase is constructed around a central column. Unlike the sweeping, curved stair, it can be used in small houses where space is limited.

Staircase with two quarter landings

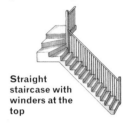

Straight staircase with winders at the top

Step to stringer joints

The treads and risers of a typical staircase are set in mortises routed into the face of a closed stringer and secured with glued wedges. The wedges are driven in from underneath to make a tight joint.

In the case of an open stringer, the outer ends of the risers are mitered into the vertical cut edges and the treads are nailed down onto the horizontal edges. The nosing on this type of tread is continued around the end of the tread by adding a short length of molding. This molding hides the endgrain of the nosing and holds the bottom of the balusters captive.

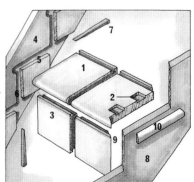

Typical stair joints
1 Tread
2 Baluster housing
3 Riser
4 Wall stringer
5 Tread groove
6 Riser groove
7 Wedge
8 Open stringer
9 Mitered butt joint
10 Molding

Newel post

In traditional stair building, the wall stringer is screwed to the wall at points underneath the treads and the outer stringer is tenoned into the newels at each end. Newel posts measure at least 4 x 4 inches. They give support to the stair while securing it to the floor and to a structural joist underneath the floor. The newel post at the top of a stairs, or the central newel on stairs with a landing, is usually continued down to the floor. The newels also carry the handrail, which is tenoned into them.

Balustrade

The space between the handrail and the outer stringer may be filled with traditional balusters, modern balustrade rails, or framed paneling. The assembly is known as the balustrade, or banister.

Storage space

In older houses, the space underneath a stair is sometimes enclosed to make a cabinet and provide extra storage room. The triangular space between the floor and the stringer can also be framed in and covered with drywall, plaster, or wood paneling. Because this filler wall is not structural, it can be removed easily in the future.

In most newer houses, the staircases between floors tend to be stacked on top of each other to make the best use of space. So it's impossible to add any storage space under the stairs.

The central stringer

Traditional stairs 3 feet wide or wider should be supported underneath by a central stringer, often called a carriage. This board is usually made of 2-inch-thick lumber that attaches to the floor plate with a birdsmouth joint, and at the top is toenailed to the side of the second-floor landing.

The width of the carriage board is determined by the distance from the corner where a tread and riser meet and the bottom of a side stringer. Short lengths of 1-inch-thick board known as carriage brackets are sometimes nailed to alternate sides of the carriage to make a tight fit under each tread and riser.

This central stringer not only helps to support the staircase, it also provides a nailing surface for any finish material, like drywall or plaster, that you might want to use to cover the underside of the stairs.

Stair components
1 Wall stringer
2 Outer stringer
3 Newel post
4 Handrail
5 Balusters
6 Wall panel
7 Carriage
8 Floor plate
9 Birdsmouth joint
10 Carriage brackets
11 Tread
12 Riser

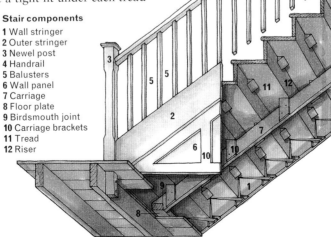

Staircase dimensions and designs are controlled by building codes, which govern tread size and shape, rise and run, minimum headroom, handrail position, and spacing of balusters. Consult your local building department before building or modifying any staircase.

Calculating the rise and run of stairs is probably the most crucial consideration, because this determines the steepness of the staircase. Most codes stipulate 8 inches as the maximum vertical distance (rise) between treads, and 9 inches as the minimum horizontal distance (run) between risers. Minimum headroom between stairs and ceiling is usually 6 feet 8 inches.

When it's properly designed, a finished staircase must fit the exact floor-to-floor height of the opening in equal stair increments. All the treads have to be level, the same size, and the same distance from the last tread. The same requirements pertain to the risers. To check staircase calculations, building inspectors often use one of these three formulas:

RISER HEIGHT + TREAD WIDTH = 17" to 18"
RISER HEIGHT x 2 + TREAD WIDTH = 24" to 27"
RISER HEIGHT x TREAD WIDTH = 70" to 75"

In these calculations, the tread width does not include the nosing (lip) that extends over the riser.

Building your own stairs
Designing and building stairs is fairly complicated, requires a lot of tools, demands a high degree of accuracy, and involves some heavy lifting. Building stairs for the inside of your house may be more than you want to tackle. But building a short run of stairs from a porch or deck to the ground is within most people's ability.

Manufactured staircases are a standard made-to-order item in lumberyards and some home centers. Accurate measurement is crucial when ordering stairs, because once they're built you have to buy them.

Curing creaking stairs

Creaking in stairs begins when joints become loose and start rubbing. The slight gaps that allow this movement are usually the result of the wood drying out and shrinking, though general wear and tear will also contribute to the problem.

The method you choose for dealing with the problem will depend on whether you have access to the underside of the stairs. A better repair is possible from underneath. But if your stairs are covered, and getting access would mean removing a ceiling, it makes more sense to tackle the repair from above.

Working from underneath

If it's possible to get to the underside of the stairs, have someone walk slowly up the steps, counting them out loud. From your position under the stairs, follow the counting, noting any loose steps and marking them with chalk or a crayon. Have your helper repeatedly step on and off any suspect treads while you look for the source of the creaking.

Loose housing joint

If the tread or the riser is loose in either stringer mortise, it may be because the original wedge has become loose. Remove the wedge **(1)**, clean it up, apply carpenter's glue, and drive the wedge back into the joint **(2)**. If you damaged the wedge when you removed it, make a new one out of hardwood.

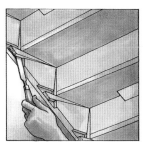

1 Pry out old wedge with chisel

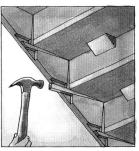

2 Apply glue to joint and drive in wedge

3 Pry open joint and squeeze in glue

4 Install glued blocks into corner joint

Loose blocks

Check the triangular blocks that fit in the corner between the tread and the riser. If the glue has failed on one side of the block, remove it and clean off the old glue. Before replacing the blocks, try to pry slightly open the joint between the tread and riser with a chisel. Squeeze glue into the joint **(3)**, then draw the joint tight by driving 1½-inch screws through the tread and into the riser.

Apply new glue to any blocks you removed and press them into the corner **(4)**. Hold the blocks in place with masking tape until the glue sets. Avoid walking on the stairs for a couple of hours to give the glue a chance to dry.

Working from the top

To identify the problem areas, walk slowly up the stairs and stop at each creaking step. Shift your weight back and forth on the problem tread to discover which part is moving. It is best to do this late at night or early in the morning, when the house is quiet and small creaks will not be missed.

Loose front joint

To cure looseness in a joint between the riser and the tread, drill clearance holes for 1½-inch screws in the tread, centered on the thickness of the riser **(1)**. Countersink the hole for the screwhead. Squeeze wood glue into the holes, then drive the screws to pull the joint tight. If the screws won't be concealed by stair carpet you should counterbore the holes and plug them with matching wood.

Loose back joint

A loose joint at the back of the tread cannot be easily repaired from above. You can try working glue into the joint. But because you can't use screws to draw the joint, the glue doesn't usually do much good.

There is a form of reinforcement from above that may help. Glue a piece of ½ x ½-inch triangular wood into the corner between the tread and the riser **(2)**. This technique is appropriate only on wide treads, where the addition of the molding doesn't reduce the tread depth to less than the minimum allowed by code, which is usually 9 inches. Cut the piece

of wood slightly shorter than the width of the stair carpet. If you have wall-to-wall carpet on the stairs, this repair doesn't make as much sense. To remove the carpet and install the block is difficult. It's probably easier to live with the creak.

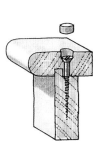

1 Screw joint tight

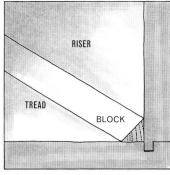

RISER

TREAD

BLOCK

2 Glue triangular block into corner

Repairing worn stairs

Old wood stairs that haven't had the protection of a floorcovering will eventually become very worn. Worn treads can be dangerous and should be repaired promptly. If all the treads are badly worn, consider having the entire staircase replaced.

Treads installed between closed stringers can be replaced only from below. If the stairs are covered underneath with drywall or plaster, you will have to cut an opening to reach the worn tread. If a central stringer has been used in the construction of the stairs the work required to repair the tread can be so extensive that you should consider hiring a contractor for the job.

Renewing a tread

Wear on the nosing of a tread is usually concentrated in the center, and you can repair it without having to replace the whole tread.

Mark three cutting lines just outside the worn area. Draw one line parallel to the edge of the nosing and draw the other two lines at right angles to it (**1**).

Adjust the blade depth of a portable circular saw to the thickness of the tread. Tack a strip parallel to edge of the tread, to guide the shoe of the saw.

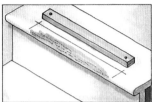

1 Mark cutting lines around worn area

2 Make the cut with saw guided by a strip

Cutting out
Position the saw, turn it on, then make the cut by lowering the blade into the wood (**2**). Try not to overrun the short end lines. Once the cut is made, remove the guide strip. Cut the end lines with a handsaw at a 45-degree angle. Make sure you don't cut beyond the saw kerf left by the circular saw. Make these cuts with a tenon saw (**3**).

You will be left with uncut waste in the corners. Remove most of the cut waste with a chisel, working with the grain and taking care to avoid damaging the riser tongue and triangular reinforcing blocks. Pare away the remaining waste from the uncut corners using a sharp chisel (**4**).

3 Make 45-degree cuts at each end

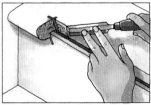

4 Pare away waste from corners

Replacement
Buy a new stair tread that matches the thickness and species of the existing tread. Then cut a groove for the riser on the underside of the new tread and cut a repair piece to length and width from the new tread. Check its fit in the opening, then apply wood glue to all of the meeting surfaces and press the repair piece in place. Clamp it down with a strip screwed at each end of the tread (**5**). Place a shim under the strip to hold down the middle of the patch (a piece of polyethylene prevents the shim from sticking to the patch). Drill and insert ¼-inch dowels into the edge of the nosing to reinforce the butt joint and, when the glue is set, plane and sand the repair flush.

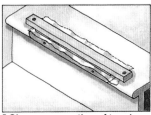

5 Clamp new section of tread with strip

Most stairs have tongue-and-groove joints between the risers and treads. In some others the top of the riser is not machined; it's left square and fits into a matching groove in the tread. In still other stairs, the risers simply butt against the treads and are held in place with nails or screws.

You can determine which type of joint you have by trying to pass a thin knife blade through the joint. Be sure to remove any nails or screws. A butt joint will let the blade pass through, while a tongue-and-groove, or a simple groove joint, will not.

As the joints effectively lock the treads and risers together, those in contact with the damaged tread must be freed before the tread can be removed. A butt joint is relatively easy to take apart; a groove or tongue-and-groove joint will have to be cut.

Dismantling a butt joint
To take a butt joint apart, first take out the nails or screws and, if glue has been used, strike the tread several times with a hammer to break the hardened glue, then pry up the tread with a chisel. Remove the triangular glue blocks in the same way.

Cutting a tongue
Where the tongue of a riser is joined to the underside of a tread, you cut it working from the front of the stair; where the riser's tongue is joined to the top of the tread, it must be cut from the rear (**1**). If there is a molding installed under the nosing (the part of the tread that extends beyond the riser), pry it off first with a chisel.

1 Cut the tongue from the front or rear.

Before cutting a tongue, remove any screws, nails, and glued reinforcement blocks, then drill a row of ⅛-inch holes into the joint to provide access for a hacksaw or keyhole-saw blade (**2**). You can also use a power reciprocating saw to make this cut, which would speed up the job.

Once the riser-to-tread joints are cut, remove the tread as shown on the facing page.

2 Start the cut with a backsaw blade

Closed stringer stairs

Working from the underside of the stair, chisel out the tread-retaining wedges from the stringer mortises at the ends of the tread **(1)**. Then free the tread by striking its front edge with a hammer and block. Continue to drive the tread backward and out **(2)**.

Make a tread to fit, shaping its front edge to match the nosing on the other steps, and cut a new pair of wedges. Slide the new tread and wedges into place from underneath. Then measure the gaps left between the risers and the tread and cut wood-shim pieces to match. Test these shims to make sure they fill the joints **(3)**.

Remove the shims, wedges, and tread. Apply wood glue to all parts as you reinstall them. Secure the tread with 1½-inch countersunk woodscrews driven into the risers.

 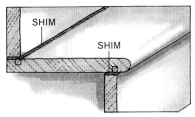

1 Remove wedges   **2 Drive out tread**   **3 Shim saw cuts at front and back**

Open stringer stairs

Pry off the molding that covers the endgrain of the tread, taking care not to split it **(1)**. Remove the two balusters from the tread.

Chisel the wedge out of the wall stringer mortise to free the inner end of the tread and drive the tread out from the rear of the stair with a hammer and a block of wood **(2)**.

You will have to cut through or extract any nails that fasten the tread to the outer stringer before the tread can be pulled completely clear.

Use the original tread as a template and mark its shape out on a new board. Then cut the board carefully to size and shape. Be sure to duplicate the shape of the nosing exactly so the return molding on the end of the tread will match all the others in the staircase.

Lay out and cut the mortises for the balusters **(3)** and make a new wedge for the wall stringer mortise. Apply glue to all the parts, then install the tread from the front, shimming the joints with the riser as described above.

Apply glue to the balusters and replace them. Then glue and nail the return molding to the end of the tread. Also replace the molding piece under the tread nosing if one was used before.

 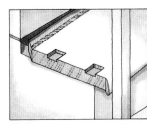

2 Drive out tread from behind

1 Pry off return molding   **3 Cut baluster housings in new tread**

Risers are subjected to much less wear and tear than treads and will not ordinarily have to be replaced. If a riser is split, it can be reinforced from behind by gluing and screwing a new board to the back of the riser. The joining surfaces of both the old and the new wood should be sanded smooth for the glue to hold well. If a riser is broken, you have no alternative; it must be replaced.

Closed stringer stair
In the case of a closed stringer stair, remove the tread below the damaged riser using the method described earlier. Knock the wedges out of the riser mortises, then drive out or pry out the riser **(1)**.

Measure the distance between the stringers and between the bottom of one tread to the top of the other. Cut a new riser to fit. Though you could make tongue-and-groove joints on the new riser, it is easier simply to butt-join its top and bottom edges with the treads **(2)**. Apply glue to all joining surfaces, then wedge the new riser into the mortises **(3)**, and screw it to the tread.

If your stairs are not covered with carpet, counterbore the screw holes and use wood plugs to conceal the screws. You can also secure a riser to a tread by gluing and screwing blocks to both parts from underneath.

Reinstall the tread you removed as described earlier (see left). In this case, you won't have to shim the riser and tread joint because the new riser has been cut to fit.

1 Pry out riser

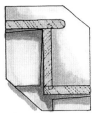

2 Cut riser to fit

3 Wedge riser

Open stringer stairs
First remove any molding that's installed under the nosing. Then saw through the joints at the top and bottom of the damaged riser. Remove the wedges from the riser's wall stringer mortise.

Knock apart the mitered joint between the end of the riser and the outer stringer by hammering it from behind. Once the mitered joint is free, carefully pry the inner end of the riser out of its mortise.

Make a new riser to fit between the treads, mitering its outer end to match the joint in the stringer. Cut any necessary shims to size. Then apply glue to all edges of the riser and the shims, and install these parts. Drive the riser wedge into the stringer mortise, screw the treads to the riser, nail the mitered end, and replace the nosing molding.

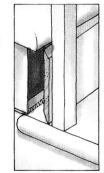

Free the mitered joint

Repairing balusters

Handrail regulations

A broken baluster is potentially dangerous and should be repaired or replaced promptly. If the baluster is a decorative one, it should be preserved. If the damage is not too extensive, it can be repaired in place. Otherwise, a new baluster should be made to replace it.

Buying and installing balusters

Finished balusters of various patterns are available from building suppliers and they can be used for replacing all the old balusters when you are replacing the entire balustrade. They can also be used to replace individual balusters if you can find ones that match your staircase. If you can't find a match, then you'll have to make, or hire someone to make, replacements. Balusters are mortised into the underside of the handrail and in the edge of a closed stringer or the treads of an open stringer. Sometimes they are simply butted and secured with nails or are set in mortises at the bottom but nailed at the top (see below). You can detect nails by examining or feeling the surface of the baluster at the back.

You will find a slight bump or hollow. If the wood is stripped, the nail will be obvious. A light shone across the joint can also reveal a nail.

Balusters
A range of typical hardwood and softwood balusters.

A period staircase with turned balusters

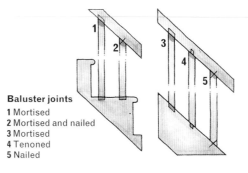

Baluster joints
1 Mortised
2 Mortised and nailed
3 Mortised
4 Tenoned
5 Nailed

Building codes require handrails on all staircases. Usually, if the staircase is narrower than 40 inches, you need only one handrail. But if it's wider, most codes demand two handrails.

If the staircase is less than 40 inches wide and has any tapered treads (winders), a handrail must be provided on the side of the stairs where the treads are widest. If this happens to be the wall stringer side, two handrails may be required, one mounted on the wall, the other as part of the balustrade.

Although these requirements govern new work, there's good reason to retrofit existing stairs to comply with them. Tapered treads, in particular, can be very hazardous, especially for children, who tend to run up and down stairs.

Repairing a baluster

Apply glue and masking tape to split baluster

A baluster that has split along the grain can be repaired in place. Work wood glue into the split and clamp it with masking tape until it dries.

Before clamping the parts with tape, squeeze the joint together and wipe away any surplus glue with a damp rag.

Replacing a baluster

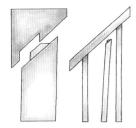

1 Trim back corner of tenon   **2 Swing into place**

A damaged baluster that is butted and nailed can be knocked out by first removing the nails, then driving its top end backward and its bottom end forward. If it is mortised at the bottom, it can be pulled out of the housing once the top has been freed.

A baluster that's mortised at both ends can be removed by cutting through the joint under the handrail and pulling the baluster from the bottom mortise.

When the baluster is installed in an open stringer, remove the molding that covers the end of the tread and knock the bottom end of the baluster sideways. Then pull it down to remove it from the handrail mortise.

Installing a baluster
Mark the required length on the new baluster and cut the ends, using the old baluster as a pattern. Install the new baluster in the reverse order of the way you took the old one out.

To replace a baluster that is mortised at both ends in a closed stringer stair, first trim off the back corner of the top tenon (1). Then push the bottom of the baluster into the bottom mortise and swing the top end of the baluster into place (2). Secure both ends with nails driven at an angle into the joints.

Installing a handrail

Fixing a loose balustrade

Measuring and marking

Mark a line on the wall to represent the top of the handrail, setting the height in accordance with building code regulations. Where there are tapered treads, some alterations of the rules may be necessary, but you should check with your local building inspector.

Lay out the line by marking a series of points measured vertically from the nosing of each tread in a straight flight. Where tapered treads occur, take the same measurement from the middle tapered tread and the landing (1).

Marking tips

Marking the points can be simplified by first cutting a straight wood strip to the right height and then using it as a guide. Circle the points with your pencil as you make them so that you can find them easily later.

Marking the handrail

Using a straightedge, join the marks to produce the line of the handrail. Then draw a second line below and parallel to the first, at a distance equal to the thickness of the handrail. Where the rail changes direction, draw lines across the intersections (A) to establish the angles at which the components must be cut (2).

Measure the run of the handrail and buy the required lengths, including any special sections required to make turns. Also buy enough handrail brackets for spacing them at 32-inch intervals.

1 Laying out
Mark the wall above each tread and join the marks with a straightedge.

2 Changing angles
The junction of a sloping handrail with a horizontal one can be made with a ramp (left) or a simple angle (right).

Assembling and installing

Cut the components to the correct lengths and angles, then dowel and glue short sections together or use special handrail bolts. These bolts require clearance holes in the ends of each of the joining parts and mortises cut in the underside of the handrail for the nuts. When using handrail bolts, you must also install dowels (3) to keep the sections from rotating as they are pulled together. Assemble the rail in manageable sections.

Screw the brackets to the rail and have a helper hold it against the wall while you mark the mounting holes. On masonry walls, drill bracket holes in the wall for wall anchors. Insert the anchors and tighten the brackets to the wall with screws (4). On wood-frame walls, locate the brackets so they fall over the studs, then attach the brackets by driving the mounting screws into the studs.

When the whole balustrade, including the handrail, balusters, and newel post, feels loose, it indicates a failure of the joints between the steps and the outer stringer. This should be addressed promptly before it get worse. If the stringer breaks, the repair is very involved and can be costly.

You can reattach the steps to a loose stringer and newel post by first removing the wedges from the tread and riser mortises. Then, working along the face of the stringer with a hammer and wood block, knock the stringer back into place to reseat the joints (1). If the stringer tends to spring away, hold it in place with a board braced between the stringer and the closest wall (2). Make new wedges, apply glue, and drive them into place to tighten the joints.

Reinforce the joint between the bottom step and the newel post by screwing metal angle plates into the corners (3).

Handrail components
In addition to ordinary handrail moldings, you can buy special matched components called turns, ramps, and caps. These are joined to straight sections of handrail with steel bolts.

1 Use a hammer and block to reseat loose joints

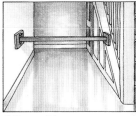

2 Brace stringer against closest wall

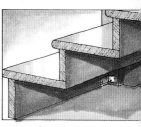

3 Reinforce bottom joint with steel angle plates

Horizontal cap turn

Horizontal turn

Opening cap

Concave ramp

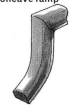

Gooseneck ramp

3 Handrails are joined with special bolts

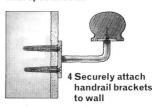

4 Securely attach handrail brackets to wall

Siding

Aluminum and vinyl

Aluminum siding comes in a number of textures and finishes, and with insulated backing laminated to it. Layout and installation is similar to that for wood. However, framed openings, corners, eaves, and other areas require special trim pieces, which often must be custom-formed using a bending brake. For this reason, most homeowners choose to have aluminum siding professionally installed.

Vinyl siding is similar to aluminum except that it doesn't bend. Preformed trim, cut to required lengths, is used at edges and openings.

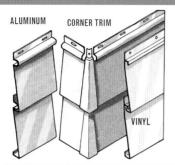

ALUMINUM   CORNER TRIM

VINYL

Unlike floor- and wall-coverings that are easier to change on a whim, siding is usually permanent, which is fortunate since replacing siding is very expensive. Wood is traditional, but the most popular siding material is vinyl because it's a maintenance-free material and it's available everywhere. But other choices can be just as appealing.

Typical siding materials

1 Vinyl lap clapboard
2 Cedar shake
3 Cement board
4 Vinyl specialty panel
5 Textured Oriented Strand Board
6 Stucco
7 Steel
8 Cedar shingle
9 Cedar clapboard
10 Hardboard
11 Texture 1-11 plywood
12 Cultured stone

Wood siding

BEVELED SIDING

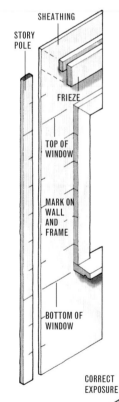

SHEATHING

STORY POLE

FRIEZE

TOP OF WINDOW

MARK ON WALL AND FRAME

BOTTOM OF WINDOW

Wood beveled siding, often called clapboards, appears on countless houses across the country. While its popularity has been eclipsed over the last 30 years by aluminum and vinyl versions, it's still used on many new homes. When installed and maintained properly, it can last well over 100 years.

Beveled siding is made from many different wood species including pine, cedar, and redwood. The boards are wedge-shaped; when installed, the thicker edge is on the bottom.

Layout

Plan the siding layout carefully to achieve a uniform exposure around windows, doors, and soffits. For a good appearance and to minimize leaks, try to align the lower edges of the boards with the tops of window and doorframes.

Use a straight length of lumber for a story pole (see left). Mark the heights of all windows and doors. Then, starting at the window and door markings, lay out the story pole with marks for each piece of siding at the recommended exposure (the amount of each siding board that's exposed to the weather). If necessary, expand or decrease the exposure slightly to get the best layout. When satisfied, transfer the story-pole marks to the wall sheathing and the window and door-trim pieces. Also make an exposure guide (see below) from a piece of scrap wood. Use it to align each board as you nail it into place.

Attaching siding

Make sure all the trim boards at the corners and around the windows and doors are installed. Then snap a chalkline for the bottom of the first board. Nail a ½ x 1½-inch primed lumber starter strip along the bottom of the sheathing ½ inch above the chalkline. Beginning at a corner, nail the bottom course of siding flush, by driving siding nails just above the filler strip. Continue all the way around the house, then snap another line to connect the next set of story-pole marks. Attach the second course of siding, checking the alignment of the boards by holding the exposure gauge against the piece of siding below. Continue all the way up the house. Caulk all the siding joints.

Windows and doors

At some window and door openings you may have to notch siding to fit. Carefully measure and mark the siding piece, then cut it with a handsaw or sabre saw. Prime the cut, nail the board in place, and caulk around the opening. Follow the same procedure for notching around all obstructions.

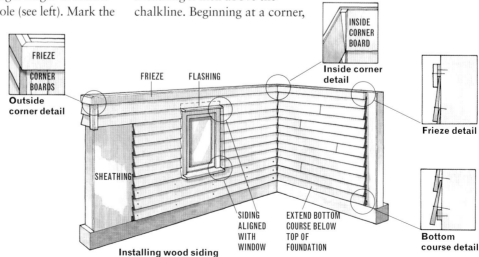

CORRECT EXPOSURE

EXPOSURE GAUGE

Calculating exposure

FRIEZE

CORNER BOARDS

Outside corner detail

FRIEZE   FLASHING

SHEATHING

SIDING ALIGNED WITH WINDOW

EXTEND BOTTOM COURSE BELOW TOP OF FOUNDATION

Installing wood siding

INSIDE CORNER BOARD

Inside corner detail

Frieze detail

Bottom course detail

Masonry siding

Mix only as much stucco as you can use in an hour. Keep mixing tools and equipment thoroughly washed so that no mortar sets on them. When you are done, hose down the work area.

Measuring

Measure level bucketfuls of sand onto a mortarboard or a sheet of exterior-grade plywood placed on the ground. Using a second dry bucket and shovel, measure out the cement, tapping the bucket to settle the loose powder and topping it up as needed.

Mixing

1 Mix sand and cement together by shoveling them from one heap to another and back again until the mix takes on a uniform gray color.

2 Form a well in the center of the heap and pour in some water.

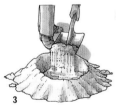

3 Shovel the dry mix from the sides of the heap into the water until the water is absorbed. If you are left with dry material, add more water as you go until you achieve firm, plastic consistency and even color.

4 If after turning the mix it is still relatively dry, sprinkle it with water. But remember that too much water will weaken the mix.

5 Draw the back of your shovel across the stucco with a sawing action to test its consistency. The ribs formed by this action should not slump or crumble, which would indicate that it is either too wet or too dry. The back of the shovel should leave a smooth texture on the surface of the stucco.

Veneer

Brick and stone veneer, used as siding, do not bear any structural load. To apply a masonry veneer, the house foundation must have a ledge in front of the wall framing wide enough to build on. First install metal flashing atop the ledge, extending 6 inches up behind the sheathing. Then attach 15-pound roofing felt to the sheathing. Nail metal masonry ties 2 to 3 feet apart horizontally and 15 inches vertically. Erect the wall, leaving a ¼-inch airspace between it and the sheathing, and anchor the masonry material to the ties as you go.

Stucco

Stucco is a mixture of portland cement and sand. It can be applied directly over brick, stone, or rough-surfaced concrete. Over wood or old siding, first install roofing felt and furring strips, then nail sheets of metal lath onto the furring. Self-furring lath is also available. Check your options at a local masonry supply outlet.

Apply stucco in three layers. To mix the first, or scratch, coat, add 1 part cement to 3 parts sand. Press generous amounts of this scratch mix into the lath with a trowel. When a layer ⅛ inch thick covers the lath, lightly rake it with a leaf rake to groove the surface. Let the basecoat stand two days, spraying frequently with water to prevent too-rapid drying.

To mix the second, or brown, coat, blend in 1-2 parts additional sand. Apply it as you did the first, in a ⅛-inch-thick layer. Roughen the surface slightly. Keep moist for two days, then allow to dry for at least five days more. For the finish, coat, most DIYers purchase a dry, premixed stucco that contains lime to make the mix smooth and workable. Apply the finish coat in a thin layer, smoothing it with a piece of straight lumber.

Applying stucco
1 Set up a safe work platform.
2 Attach furring and lath.
3 Apply scratch coat and groove with rake.
4 Apply brown coat and roughen lightly.
5 Apply finish coat.

Stucco patch repairs

Stucco should be applied with a metal plasterer's trowel and the topcoat finished with a wooden float. Start by taking a trowelful of mortar and spread it on the wall with firm pressure, applying it with an upward stroke (**1**).

Build up the undercoat layer so it's no more than two-thirds the thickness of the original stucco or ⅛ inch, whichever is thinner. Level the mortar with a straight strip of wood that fits within the area being patched. Move the strip from side to side. Then scratch grooves in the surface for the topcoat (**2**). Let the undercoat set for a few days.

Finish coat

Before applying, dampen the undercoat. Once you've troweled the stucco onto the wall, level it with a straightedge laid across the surfaces of the surrounding stucco. Work from the bottom to the top of the patch, with a side-to-side motion.

1 Use firm pressure

2 Groove surface

Roofs

Traditionally most roofs were made with rafters that were cut and installed on site, and this is still the way many roofs are built, especially when usable attic space is required. But most roofs today are built with trusses. These units are fabricated in factories and simply nailed in place on site. Trusses are strong, stable, and usually more economical than rafter roofs. But installing them generally eliminates the attic space.

Basic construction

The framework of an ordinary roof is based on a triangle, the most rigid and economical form for a loadbearing structure. The weight of the roofing and sheathing is carried either by prefabricated trusses, or by framing members called rafters, which are installed in opposing pairs. Rafters are joined at the top to a central ridge board running the length of the roof. The bottom ends of the rafters are attached to the top plates of the walls.

To stop the roof's weight from pushing the walls out, horizontal members tie the walls together and the rafters together. The bottom ones, installed next to the rafters on the top plates, are the ceiling joists. Members that are nailed to the sides of the rafters, closer to the ridge, are called collar ties.

Roof types

There are many different roof styles, often used in combination. Most of them, however, fall into these basic classifications:

Flat Roof
Flat roofs may be supported on joists to which the ceiling material is also attached, or they may be constructed using trusses, which have parallel top and bottom members supported by triangular bracing in between. Most flat roofs actually have a slight slope, formed by the roofing material, to provide drainage.

Shed Roof
This is the simplest type of roof. Sometimes it is called a lean-to roof. Inside the structure, the ceiling may be attached directly to the rafters to form a sloping surface, or be supported by horizontal joists to form a flat surface.

Gable Roof
Two shed roofs joined together form the classic gable roof, the most commonly used roof in residential construction today. Gable roofs are simple and economical to build and have excellent loadbearing and drainage capabilities. The end walls under the roof are nonloadbearing.

Gambrel Roof
By breaking the slope of a gable roof into two differently pitched sections, more headroom becomes available in the attic area beneath the rafters. The gambrel design also makes the construction of a wide roof easier because shorter lengths of lumber can be used in combination to span large widths.

Hip Roof
By sloping the ends of a gable roof toward the center, a hip roof is formed. This roof style provides a protective overhang on all four sides of the building.

Intersecting Roofs
Many houses combine the same or different roof types, built at angles to one another, to form L- or U-shaped floor plans, and other shapes.

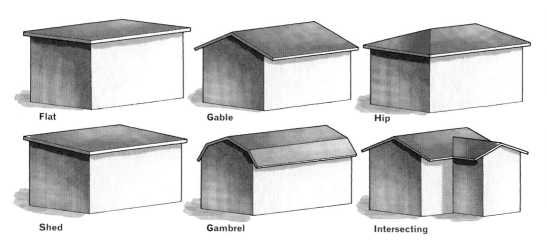

Flat   Gable   Hip

Shed   Gambrel   Intersecting

Roof construction

Gable rafter roof

A gable roof **(1)**, is the basic design for residential roof construction. It can be made with trusses (see below) or traditional rafters. Even though building a gable roof is a lot of work, its design is the essence of simplicity: Two flat planes are joined together to form a simple peaked structure.

The top of the framework is called the ridge and it is formed by the junction of the rafters from both sides and a ridge board that runs perpendicular to the rafters. The ridge is supported by the rafters and the rafters are supported by the outside walls. The joint between the rafters and the top wall plate is crucial. If this joint is weak the roof will fail.

To tie the rafters together and form the basic triangle, and to keep the walls from spreading, ceiling joists are nailed to the top plates and the sides of the rafters. These joints are also crucial to the overall strength of the roof.

Purlin roof

In a purlin roof **(2)**, horizontal beams called purlins link the rafters, running midway between the outside wall and the ridge.

The ends of the purlins are supported at the gable wall or, in the case of a hip roof, by hip rafters (see below). The purlins effectively reduce the unsupported span of the rafters, which allows relatively lightweight lumber to be used for the rafters. In order to keep the size of the purlins to a minimum, diagonal struts are installed in opposing pairs to brace them, usually every fourth or fifth rafter. The struts transfer some of the roof weight back to a center loadbearing wall. This type of roof is rarely built anymore; but looking at it suggests the beginning of truss roof construction.

Truss roof

A truss roof **(3)** allows for a relatively wide span and dispenses with the need for a loadbearing partition wall. Like rafters, trusses transfer the entire weight of the roof to the exterior walls.

In the majority of new housing, trusses are computer designed for economy and strength. Each truss combines two roof chords (corresponding to common rafters), a bottom chord (to function like a ceiling joist), and struts that join and brace the chords together. All the joints are butt joints reinforced with heavy-duty plate connectors, often called gang nails. Trusses are usually spaced on 24-inch centers so standard roof sheathing panels will fit the layout without being cut.

Truss roofs are relatively lightweight and can span greater distances than rafter roofs, because trusses don't require a partition wall underneath to support the ceiling joists.

Hip roof

Hip roofs **(4)** are often used for additions to gable roofs to break up the simplicity of a straight roof. Hips are more complicated to build because their ends are also pitched at an angle. Additional framing members include hip rafters, jack rafters, crown rafters, and cripple rafters. The points where the hip roof meets the gable roof are called valleys. The valleys collect and direct rainwater from both roof surfaces down to the gutters.

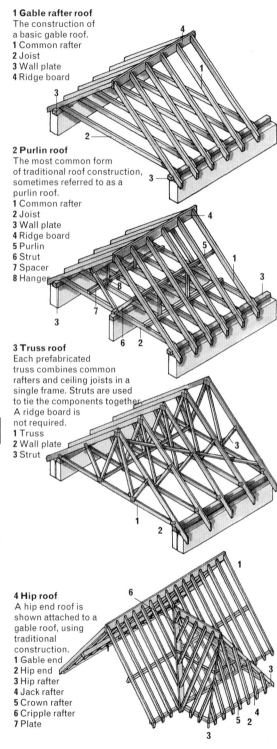

1 Gable rafter roof
The construction of a basic gable roof.
1 Common rafter
2 Joist
3 Wall plate
4 Ridge board

2 Purlin roof
The most common form of traditional roof construction, sometimes referred to as a purlin roof.
1 Common rafter
2 Joist
3 Wall plate
4 Ridge board
5 Purlin
6 Strut
7 Spacer
8 Hanger

3 Truss roof
Each prefabricated truss combines common rafters and ceiling joists in a single frame. Struts are used to tie the components together. A ridge board is not required.
1 Truss
2 Wall plate
3 Strut

4 Hip roof
A hip end roof is shown attached to a gable roof, using traditional construction.
1 Gable end
2 Hip end
3 Hip rafter
4 Jack rafter
5 Crown rafter
6 Cripple rafter
7 Plate

Checking your roof

The style of a roof is classified not only by the basic shape of the structure but also by the detailing along the eaves. The eaves are where the ends of the rafter meet the exterior walls. The basic eaves variations are shown below.

Flush eaves

When the ends of the rafters are cut flush with the outside wall of the house and covered with a fascia board, the eaves are called flush **(1)**. Gutters are installed directly on the fascia.

Open eaves

If the ends of the rafters extend beyond the outside of the wall, and aren't covered with a fascia board, the eaves are referred to as open **(2)**. This style of eaves is no longer very popular in new construction. But many older houses have them, and frequently the ends have designs cut or carved in them. Gutters are usually in brackets nailed to the top of the rafters before the roofing is installed.

Closed eaves

A closed eave **(3)** is a combination of the flush and the open approaches. The rafters extend past the outside wall, like open eaves. But they are enclosed with a fascia board, like a flush eave. A soffit board is installed under the rafters to close the space.

Eaves vents
Various types of vents are available for installing in fascias and soffits.

1 Flush eaves

2 Open eaves

3 Closed eaves

A well-constructed roof will give many years of service

A roof structure can fail if its members are exposed to high moisture levels and insect attacks. Failure can also result from overloading due to the use of undersized framing lumber, roofing that's too heavy for the structure, or modifications to the framework to add stairs, dormers, or an attic room without proper reinforcement. A sagging roof, which indicates serious damage, can usually be seen from the ground.

Inspecting your roof

Inspect the roof from inside. Do this annually to check for any leaks and the presence of destructive insects. For the inspection to be useful, you must have a good source of light. If your attic has no lighting, use an extension cord with a lamp or work light on the end. If the attic has no floor, walk only on the top edges of the joists.

Moisture problems

Rot in roof members is a serious problem which should be corrected by professionals. Rot is caused by damp conditions that encourage the growth of desctructive fungi.

Inspect the roof sheathing for loose or damaged boards or panels near the rot. Remember that water may be penetrating the roof at a higher level and running down to the rotted area. The source of water damage is not always obvious.

If the rot is close to the intersection of two roofs, suspect the flashing. Rot can also be caused by too much condensation in the roof space, a problem that's usually fixed by installing more ventilation.

You should also inspect all the openings in the roof to make sure water isn't leaking around them. This includes the main plumbing vent stack, roof vents, and chimneys. If they're accessible, check the eaves for evidence that water has backed up due to ice dams or clogged downspouts. Many older homes have windows in the attic that should be checked for leaks and faulty glazing.

Strengthening the roof

A roof that shows signs of sagging may have to be jacked and braced. But some sagging roofs have already been stabilized, so they don't present a structural problem. They may look bad but aren't in any danger of collapsing. In some old buildings a slightly sagging roof line is even considered attractive.

Consult an engineer if you suspect a roof is weak. Apart from a sagging roofline, the walls under the eaves should be inspected for bulging out of plumb. Bulging can occur where improperly framed window openings are close to the eaves, making that section of the wall weak. The walls can also bulge because the roof weight is spreading them apart. This is almost always the result of poor joints between the rafters and the ceiling joists.

A lightly constructed roof can be made stronger by adding extra structural members. This work can often be done from inside the attic. But when the damage is severe, the roofing and sheathing have to be stripped from the outside before the repairs can be made.

This is work for professionals. Make sure they have liability insurance before hiring them.

Underlayment

New roof sheathing, and sheathing that's been stripped of old roofing, should be covered with 15-pound asphalt felt paper, as underlayment, before new roofing is installed. Felt paper prevents the passage of moisture from outside in but doesn't prevent water vapor from inside getting out. Some roofers prefer to use 30-pound felt paper as underlayment. Never use plastic sheeting for underlayment.

Most roofers cover the entire roof with underlayment before installing the roofing because of the extra protection it affords a wood roof in case of rain. But because wind easily damages thin felt paper, you may want to apply underlayment in stages.

Before you install the felt paper, you need to install a drip edge along the roof eaves. A stock item at building suppliers, drip edging is easy to cut with tinsnips and is nailed to the sheathing with roofing nails. Some roofers also install metal edging, sometimes called rake edge, over the ends of the roof where the sheathing meets the rake trim.

Once the edging is in place, apply the underlayment. Be sure the sheathing surface is dry, smooth, and free of protruding nails and splinters. Apply roofing cement to the upper surface of the drip edge and along the seam where it meets the sheathing. Then set the roll of felt at one end of the roof and unroll it across the roof. Keep it about ¼ inch above the bottom of the drip edge.

Staple or nail the paper to the decking in as few places as possible, just enough to hold it until the new roofing can be applied on top. Lap the next course of paper 2 inches over the first course; overlap 4 inches at vertical seams.

At roof or hip ridges, fold the paper over the peak from both sides to produce a double thickness. Also overlap the paper at the valleys to produce a double thickness there. Install the valley flashing and all other flashings, around chimneys and vents, on top of the felt.

Applying three-tab asphalt shingles

Types of asphalt shingles

The most common type of asphalt shingles are the three-tab variety. These shingles usually measure 3 feet long and 1 foot wide. The length is divided into three sections, called tabs, that are each about 1 foot wide. Other types of asphalt shingles are available. There are strip shingles which have no tabs, interlocking shingles that hook into each other so they're less prone to wind damage, and the newer architectural shingles that have a series of overlapping tabs that are meant to simulate slate and cedar shingle roofing. When properly installed, all these shingles work well.

Installing shingles

To install three-tab shingles, begin shingling at the eaves. First install a single course of full-length shingles, top-edge down, along the length of the roof. Use roofing nails to attach them. Extend the shingles ¼ inch beyond the bottom edge of the drip edge. Then nail a second layer of full-size shingles top edge up over the first layer to complete the starter course.

So that the cutouts in each shingle will always center over the tabs in the course below, remove half a tab from the first shingle that starts the second course. Attach the shingle so that

5 to 6 inches of the shingle beneath are exposed. This exposure varies depending on the shingles you buy. Follow the manufacturer's directions for the proper exposure.

Lay the rest of the course, nailing about ⅝ inch above each cutout and within 1 inch of both ends. Space subsequent shingles to provide the same exposure as used on the first course. After completing the second course, start the third, removing an entire tab from the first shingle in the course.

Mark where the upper edge of the next course of shingles will fall on both ends of the roof. Snap a chalkline between these two marks. Then lay the shingles in the next course to this line. Snap a line for each ensuing course and continue until you reach the ridge. Install shingles in the same way on the other side of the roof.

Installing the ridge cap

Trim the last row of shingles to lie flat along the ridge. Cover their top edges with a ridge cap made of individual shingle tabs. To do this, first snap a chalkline on each side of the roof, 5½ inches below the ridge. Fold the tabs over the ridge and align them with the chalklines. Nail the caps in place, maintaining the same exposure you used for the rest of the roof.

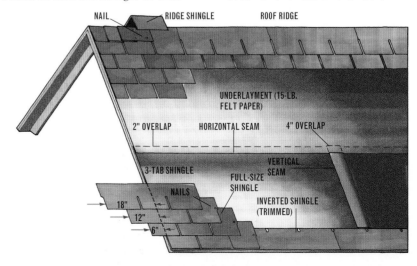

NAIL · RIDGE SHINGLE · ROOF RIDGE · UNDERLAYMENT (15-LB. FELT PAPER) · 2" OVERLAP · HORIZONTAL SEAM · 4" OVERLAP · VERTICAL SEAM · 3-TAB SHINGLE · FULL-SIZE SHINGLE · NAILS · INVERTED SHINGLE (TRIMMED) · 18" · 12" · 6"

Roof maintenance and repairs: slate roofs

● **Inspecting a slate roof**

● **Inspecting a slate roof**
The roofs of older houses should be checked at least once a year. Start by taking a look at the roof from ground level. Usually, loose or askew slates can be spotted easily against the regular lines of the rest of the roofing. The color of any newly exposed slate will also indicate damage.

Look at the ridge against the sky to check for misalignment and gaps in the joints. Make a closer inspection with binoculars, focusing on all the flashing around chimneys, vents, and roof windows.

From inside an unfinished attic, you will be able to spot daylight through breaks in the slate. Also check the roof framing for water stains, which would indicate failure in the roofing or the flashing.

Roof coverings have a limited life, the length depending on the quality of materials used, the installation workmanship, and the exposure to severe weather. An average asphalt shingle roof can be expected to last for 20 years. But some materials, like slate and clay tiles, can last for 100 years or more. Of course, proper maintenance will always extend longevity, no matter what type of material is installed on your roof.

Slate roofs

During the long life of a slate roof, patching can become a regular maintenance chore. But there comes a time when it simply makes more sense to start over. If you have to replace a slate roof, you're in for a big, expensive job, and any way to cut the costs is welcome. One strategy is to remove the old slate carefully so some of it can be reused. For example, you may want new slate installed on the front side of the roof, but be willing to live with the older slate installed on the back side or on a garage roof. If the slate is carefully removed, you may also be able to sell it in bulk to roofing companies that specialize in restoration work. Reinstalling a slate roof is definitely a job for an experienced roofing contractor who has good references.

Removing and replacing a slate

A slate may slip out of place because the nails have corroded or because the slate itself has broken. Whatever the cause, loose or broken slates should be replaced as soon as possible, before a high wind strips them off the roof.

Use a ripper to remove the trapped part of a broken slate. Slip the ripper under the slate and locate its hooked end over one of the nails **(1)**. Then pull down hard on the tool to extract or cut through the nail. Remove the second nail in the same way.

Even where an old slate has already fallen out completely, you still need to remove the nails so you can install the replacement slate.

You will not be able to nail a new slate in place. Instead, use a 1-inch-wide copper strip or a plastic clip designed for holding replacement slates in place. Attach the strip to the roof by driving a nail between the slates of the lower course **(2)**, then slide the new slate into position and turn back the end of the strip to secure it **(3)**.

1 Pull out nails

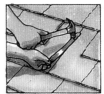

2 Nail strip to roof

3 Fold strip over slate

Cutting slates and tiles

Cut slate with trowel

Cutting roof tiles with an angle grinder
Follow scored guideline with cutting disc.

Cutting slates
You may have to cut a slate to fit the gap in your roof. With a sharp point, scratch a cutline on the back of the slate. Then place the slate beveled side down on a bench or sawhorse. Hold the slate so the cutline is over the edge of the work surface. Then chop the slate with the edge of a mason's trowel. You can also use a rented slate cutter. It works like a pair of sheetmetal snips. Either drill nail holes or punch them out with a masonry nail. A punched hole leaves a recess for the head of a roofing nail.

Cutting cement slates
Having scribed deep lines, break a cement tile over a straightedge or cut it to size with a circular saw outfitted with a masonry-cutting blade. If you saw cement slates, wear a dust mask and goggles. These slates are relatively brittle, so bore nail holes with a drill.

Cutting tiles
If you need to cut roof tiles, either use an abrasive blade in a circular saw or rent an angle grinder for the purpose. Always wear protective goggles and a dust mask when cutting tile.

Replacing a roof tile

Individual tiles can be difficult to remove because of the the retaining nibs on their back edges and their interlocking shape.

To remove a plain tile that is broken, lift the nibs clear of the board that it rests on, then pull the tile out. This is easier if the overlapping tiles are first raised on wood wedges inserted at both sides of the tile **(1)**. If the tile is also nailed, try rocking it loose. If this fails, you will have to break it out carefully. You may then have to use a ripper to extract or cut any remaining nails.

Use a similar technique for a single-lap interlocking tile, but in this case you will also have to wedge up the tile to the left of the one being removed **(2)**. If the tile has a deep profile, you will have to ease up a number of surrounding tiles to achieve the required clearance.

If you are removing tiles in order to install something, such as a roof vent, then you can afford to break the one you're replacing. Use a hammer to crack it, taking care not to damage adjacent tiles. The remaining tiles should be easier to remove once the first is taken out.

1 Lift the overlapping tiles with wedges

2 Lift interlocking tiles above and to the left

Installing ridge tiles

When the old mortar breaks down, a whole row of ridge tiles can be left with practically nothing but their weight holding them in place.

Lift off the ridge tiles and clear all the crumbling mortar from the roof and from the undersides of the tiles. Be sure to soak the tiles in water before reinstalling them.

Mix 1 part cement and 3 parts sand to make a stiff mortar. Load a bucket about half full and carry it onto the roof. Dampen the top courses of the roof tiles or slates and lay a thick bed

of mortar on each side of the ridge, following the line left behind by the old mortar **(1)**. Lay mortar for one or two tiles at a time.

Press each ridge tile into the mortar, and use a trowel to slice off mortar that has squeezed out. Try not to smear any on the tile itself.

Build up a bed of mortar to fill the hollow end of each tile, inserting pieces of tile to keep the mortar from slumping **(2)**. Install the rest of the tiles the same way.

1 Apply bed of mortar on both sides of ridge

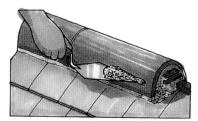

2 Insert pieces of tile to stabilize mortar

Working on a roof can be hazardous, and if you are unsure of yourself when working high off the ground, you should hire a contractor to do the work. If you do decide to do it yourself, it's best not to use ladders alone for roof repairs. Rent sectional scaffolding and scaffolding boards to provide a safe working platform.

All roofing materials are fragile, to a certain extent. Masonry roofing like slate, clay, and concrete tiles can break easily. Wood shingles and shakes get brittle over time. And even common asphalt roofing can be easily damaged, especially if you walk over it on a hot sunny day when the shingles are soft from the heat.

When you combine the possibility of roof damage with the safety issues related to working off the ground, you may wonder who would ever work on their own roof. The answer is, not many people. But there are ways to work on a roof safely that won't damage the roofing. One of the best is to use a roof ladder (see below).

Roof ladders are common rental items made with elevated rails that keep the treads clear of the roof surface and spread the load over a larger area. The top section hooks over the ridge to keep the ladder from sliding. A roof ladder should reach from the scaffold at the eaves to the ridge of the roof. Some models are equipped with wheels, so you can roll the ladder up the slope and then turn it over to engage the hook. Never leave tools on the roof when they are not being used. And keep those that are needed safely inside a tool belt or a drywall bucket hanging from the side of a ladder tread.

A roof ladder allows safe access to roof

Roof repairs: asphalt shingles

Curled shingles, or those that are slightly torn or broken off, can be repaired. Badly damaged shingles should be replaced. It's a good idea to take the weather into account before starting work. Pick a warm (but not hot) day if possible, so that shingles will be pliable but not soft to the touch. Cold stiffens asphalt shingles, causing them to crack easily.

Repairing asphalt shingles

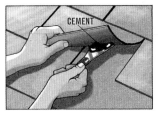

Apply a spot of roofing cement to the underside, then weight down the shingle with a brick (1). For torn shingles, apply cement liberally, press shingle down, and nail both edges. Apply roofing cement to nail holes before nailing heads down.

1 Fixing curled shingles

Cut a piece of metal flashing to size of the broken shingle (2), plus 3 inches on both sides. Apply roofing cement to underside of flashing, slide it in place beneath damaged shingle, then apply cement to top of flashing and press damaged shingle into it.

2 Repairing broken shingle

Replacing a shingle

Carefully lift the damaged shingle and pry up the nails with a flat bar (1a). Then lift the shingle above the damaged one, pull the nails, and remove the shingle. Stubborn nails that remain should be driven flush with a flat bar and hammer (1b).

Align the bottom edge of the new shingle with the edges of the adjacent shingles (2). Lift up the shingles above so you can nail the new shingle in place. Apply cement to the underside of all lifted shingles, and press them flat.

1a Prying up nails

1b Driving stubborn nails flush

2 Sliding the new shingle into place

Patching ridge shingles

Cover small damaged areas with roofing cement. If the damage is more extensive, repair with flashing as shown above or with a shingle patch (shown here). Apply cement to the damaged shingle (1). Press the patch over it, and nail all four corners (2). Apply roofing cement to nail holes before driving the heads flush, to reduce the chance of leaks around the nails.

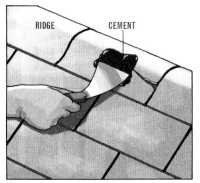

1 Applying roofing cement

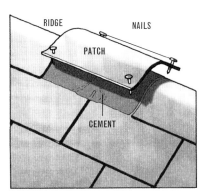

2 Placing the patch

Roof repairs: wood shingles

Thorough ventilation is the key to preserving wood shingles. Unless they can dry out after becoming wet, they will rot. Shingle roofs often have wide spaces between decking boards to allow significant airflow underneath. However, even if a solid sheathing like plywood is used, asphalt felt underlayment should never be installed between the sheathing and the shingles. If the roof has wood shakes instead of shingles, underlayment is recommended.

When you need to repair wood shingles or shakes, your first goal is to avoid causing more damage to the roof while you're working. Old wood shingles can be very brittle. The best time for shingle repair is the day after a soaking rain, when the shingles are still soft and somewhat pliable.

Access

To gain good access to the top of a broken shingle, you must lift the shingles above it with small wood wedges. Carefully drive the wedges under the good shingles until there's a gap of about ¼ inch. Then drive wedges under the bottom edge of the broken shingle to lift it slightly off the roof (**1**).

Removing the shingle

Using a chisel, split the broken shingle in several places, and pull out the waste (**2**). Split the pieces that are still held by the nails until the pieces can be pulled free.

To cut the nails, use a plain hacksaw blade with its end covered in duct tape (**3**). Cut the nails flush with the surface of the shingle below, so the new shingle will lay flat. Remove all the dust and wood chips from the repair area.

Installing the new shingles

Cut a new shingle to width so there's a ¼-inch gap on both sides. Then slide the shingle into the opening so its bottom edge lines up with the ones next to it. Remove the wedges that are holding up the shingles on the next course, and press these shingles down. Drive two nails into the replacement shingle. These should be located 1 inch in from both sides and 1 inch below the shingles above (**4**).

Making ridge repairs

Traditionally the ridge on wood roofs has been covered in two ways. One is with two boards nailed over the last course of shingles and butted together above the ridge. These boards are usually 1 x 4 cedar planks. If these boards are cracked, they should be replaced.

The other ridge-sealing method uses shingles that are nailed together in pairs to form a V-shaped cap. Each cap is nailed in place along the ridge, much like an asphalt shingle ridge cap. All the nails are covered by ensuing caps, and the exposure of the cap shingles matches the exposure on the roof. Broken cap shingles are repaired in the same way as other shingles.

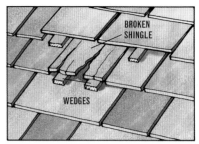

1 Using wedges
Drive wedges beneath damaged shingle and overlapping shingles in upper course.

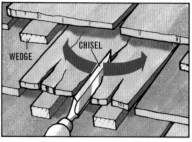

2 Removing damaged shingle
Remove damaged shingle by splitting it apart using a chisel.

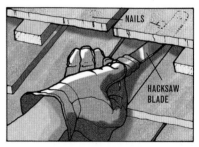

3 Sawing through nails
Saw through nails that held damaged shingle. Use a hacksaw blade wrapped with duct tape.

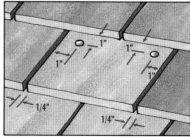

4 Installing new shingle in line with others
Leave ¼-inch gap on each side. Nail in place 1 inch from shingle edges and overlapping shingles.

Flashing

Flashing prevents water from getting under the roofing where two or more planes of a roof meet, or where the roof meets a wall. It is also used along roof edges, and around windows and doors to direct water away from the inside of the house. Flashing is also required around all vent openings.

Inspecting flashing

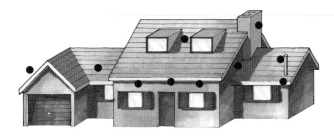

• **Flashing materials**
Roll roofing is commonly used for some flashing, particularly along valleys where two roofs meet. But the most durable flashing materials are aluminum and copper. Both are sold in rolls and rigid pieces.

Inspect flashing at least once a year. Look for cracks or other damage where the flashing meets the chimney (1), vent stack (2), wall (3), and dormer (4), where roof planes meet at valleys (5), along the rakes (6) and eaves (7), and over the windows (8) and the doors (9).

Very old flashing sometimes develops pinholes which are hard to see. These can be repaired by coating them with plastic roof cement.

Maintenance and repair

It is not a bad idea to coat all flashing seams periodically with plastic roofing cement, especially at chimneys and around vent stacks. Apply the cement using a small mason's trowel and smooth the surface of the cement so that it does not form hollows and ridges where water may collect. Where you find holes 1-square-inch or bigger, cut a patch from the same material as the flashing. Make it 1 inch larger than the hole all around. Apply cement to the damaged flashing, press the patch into place, then cover the entire area with cement and smooth the surface.

Repointing flashing

Rake out joint and repoint with fresh mortar.

Where flashing meets brick, it is usually embedded in mortar. Separations here require immediate repair since the loose flashing actually collects water and funnels it between the bricks where it can spread and do considerable damage. If the flashing itself is sound, just rake out the old mortar from the joint to a depth of about ¾ inch. Press the flashing back into place, wedging it if necessary with small stones. Then, using a trowel, fill the seam with fresh mortar. Smooth the joint carefully. After the mortar has fully cured, seal the flashing with roofing cement.

Corrosion Table
1 Aluminum
2 Zinc
3 Steel
4 Tin
5 Lead
6 Brass
7 Copper
8 Bronze

Galvanic action

Dissimilar metals touching each other react when wet. As a result, metal flashing must be fastened with nails made of the same metal as the flashing, otherwise one or the other will corrode, often quickly. If it is impossible to match flashing and fasteners, use neoprene washers with the fasteners to prevent direct contact between the two metals. The chart (right) shows common construction metals. When paired, metals farthest apart in the chart corrode soonest and fastest. Metals in contact with acid-containing woods, like redwood and cedar, can also corrode.

Chimney flashing is usually in two parts: the base, or step, flashing that wraps completely around the chimney and under the roofing, and the cap, or counter, flashing that covers the top of the base flashing.

To replace chimney flashing, use a cold chisel to carefully chip out the mortar joints that hold the cap flashing and remove it. Then chisel the joints deeper, to a depth of about 1½ inches. Remove any roof shingles or other covering that overlaps the base flashing, and carefully pry it free. Use the old flashing pieces as patterns to cut new pieces, preferably from copper sheet sold for the purpose. Bend the flashing to shape after cutting, then fasten it in place using roofing cement. Attach the front piece of base flashing first, then the sides. Fasten the back piece last.

Reinstall, or replace, the shingles that cover the base flashing. Then install the cap flashing in the same order as the base flashing: front, sides, back. Fill all the joints with fresh mortar, and when it is fully cured, seal the joints with roofing cement.

Base flashing

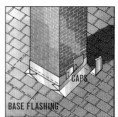

Cap flashing

Flashing repairs

Vertical wall flashing

A row of individual, overlapping flashing shingles are often installed where dormers join roofs and where a roof joins a higher house wall. To locate and repair leaks in these areas, the siding and roofing must be removed.

Look for rotten or discolored sheathing, and evidence that settling has occurred, which may have pulled house sections apart slightly. After repairing any of these problems, fill any gaps between building sections with strips of wood. Apply new felt underlayment over the wood, then reflash the area as you reshingle.

To do this, attach a flashing shingle at the end of each course, fastened to the vertical surface with one nail at the upper corner. Each flashing shingle should overlap the one underneath, and extend at least 4 inches up the adjacent wall and 2 inches under the roofing. After the flashing and the roofing are completely installed, attach new siding to cover the top edge of the flashing.

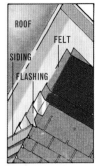

Wall flashing

Flashing a vent stack

Sometimes you may be able to stop leaks by tightening the lead collar (if one is present) around the neck of a pipe where it passes through the roof.

To do this, tap the collar with a blunt cold chisel and a hammer. Work around the upper rim of the collar, sealing it against the stack.

Also try coating the entire flashing area and lower portion of the vent stack with roofing cement. If a good repair is not possible, then you'll have to install new flashing.

Carefully remove the shingles covering the old flashing. In some cases you can just slip a new piece of flashing over the old one and replace the roofing. But in most cases, you'll have to pry up the old flashing (1), place a new piece of felt on the the roof sheathing, install the new flashing (2),. and then reinstall the roofing. The flashing should

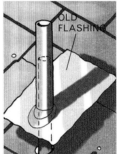

1 Remove shingles and old flashing

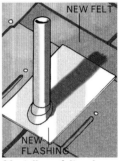

2 Install new felt and flashing

overlap the bottom shingles and fit under the top shingles.

Drip flashing
During construction, strips of flashing are installed above doors and windows and along the edges of the roof. These should extend several inches under the siding or roof covering and be nailed well away from the edges. On roofs, the drip edge goes on top of the underlayment along the rake and beneath it at the eaves. If minor repairs do not suffice, remove the siding or roof covering that overlaps the flashing. Determine the cause of the leak, then replace the drip edge, cover any seams with roofing cement, and reinstall the siding or roofing material.

Valley flashing

Where shingles are trimmed so that flashing is visible, the construction is called an open valley. When the shingles overlap the flashing, hiding it from view, it's called a closed valley.

Small repairs to open valley flashing can be made with roofing cement. Larger holes can be patched with flashing material coated on the bottom and top with roofing cement. Leaks from no apparent source may sometimes be stopped by applying a bead of cement between the edges of the trimmed shingles and the flashing.

To repair closed valley flashing, first try slipping squares of copper or aluminum flashing material underneath the shingles in the damaged area. Loosen or remove the nails closest to the valley, then bend and install the squares beginning at the bottom of the roof. Overlap them until they extend 2 inches beyond the damaged area. Renail the shingles and cover the nailheads with roofing cement. If leaks persist, remove the valley shingles and install new flashing. Then replace the shingles.

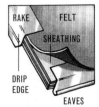

Drip edge

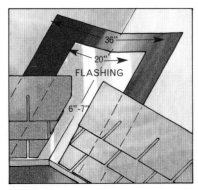

Open valley flashing

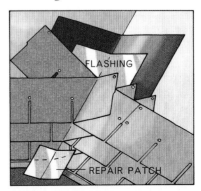

Closed valley flashing

A properly sized system of gutters and downspouts, in good working condition, constitutes basic preventive maintenance. Gutters prevent water from running down the sides of the house, causing damage and discoloration. Combined with downspouts, gutters also direct water away from the foundation of the building, lessening the risk of the basement flooding and the foundation settling. Gutters also protect flowerbeds and other landscaping around the perimeter of the house. Inspect gutters frequently.

Gutters and downspouts

Gutters are made of a number of materials. Traditional preferences were for wood or copper. Although both are still used occasionally, most gutters now are made of galvanized steel, aluminum, and vinyl. The size and layout of a gutter system must allow it to discharge all the water from the roof area it serves. The flow load required depends mainly on the area of the roof.

For roofs with areas less than 750 square feet, 4-inch-wide gutters usually suffice. Choose 5-inch gutters for roofs with areas between 750 and 1400 square feet. Six-inch gutters are available for even larger roofs.

Downspouts also should be properly sized to carry away runoff.

For roof areas up to 1000 square feet, 3-inch downspouts are usually sufficient. Larger roofs require 4-inch downspouts.

The location of downspouts can affect the system's performance. A central downspout can serve double the roof area of one with an end outlet. A right-angled bend in guttering will reduce the flow capacity by about 20 percent, if it is placed near the outlet downspout.

There are three basic types of hanging hardware for gutters see below). Although 30-inch spacing is standard, 24-inch spacing provides better support to withstand snow and ice loads.

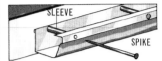

Gutter spike is driven through gutter into fascia board. Sleeve fits in trough.

Strap hanger fastens under shingle

Bracket fastens to fascia board

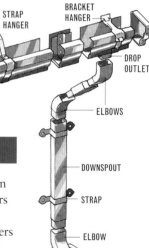

Gutter materials

Wood gutters, made of fir, redwood, or red cedar, are all decay resistant. Generally they are used with wood-shingled roofs. Wood gutters are very sturdy and if maintained will last the life of the house.

Galvanized steel gutters are often the lowest priced of all systems. Sold unfinished or enameled, they have a short life compared to other materials unless frequently repainted. Paint does not adhere well to galvanized steel unless a special primer is used to keep the new paint from flaking.

Aluminum is a very common gutter material. Available in several enamel

colors, it is lightweight and corrosion resistant. However, aluminum gutters will not withstand much ladder pressure. Sometimes aluminum gutters are formed in a continuous piece on site. But more often the systems are assembled in place, using stock components that are available in standard dimensions.

Vinyl gutters are increasingly popular. Like aluminum systems, the gutter sections and fittings come in different colors and in standard sizes. Many do-it-yourselfers find them easier to install and repair than other systems.

Repairing small holes

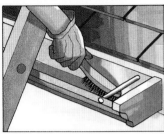

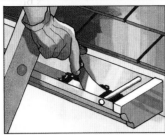

1 To repair pinholes and small rust spots
First clean the gutter and scrub the damaged area using wire brush or coarse abrasive paper. Wipe away residue using a rag dipped in paint thinner.

2 Apply coat of roofing cement
On holes larger than 1/4 inch, sandwich layers of heavy aluminum foil between coats of roofing cement. Smooth topcoat so water won't collect.

Patching large areas

CARDBOARD

1 To repair a large hole
First use thin cardboard to make a pattern, then cut a patch of the same material as the gutter to fit over the area, overlapping the hole at least 1 inch.

2 Coat with roofing cement
Press the patch into a bed of roofing cement, then crimp it over the edge of the gutter. Apply another layer of cement, smoothing it so water won't collect.

Maintaining wood gutters

Repaint wood gutters at least once every three years. Be sure to work during a period of warm, fair weather.

First clear the gutter and allow a few days for the wood to dry thoroughly. Next, sand the interior of the gutter smooth and remove the residue with a whisk broom and handheld vacuum. Wipe the sanded trough with paint thinner, then apply a thin coat of roofing cement mixed with paint thinner to brushing consistency. This helps the cement enter the pores of the wood.

After the first coat of cement has dried, wait two days, then apply a second thin coat. Sand and repaint the gutter exterior with two coats of high-quality house paint.

Inspect and clean out the interiors of gutters at least twice a year, in autumn after the leaves have fallen and again in early spring. Check more often if you live in a heavily wooded area. Use a ladder to reach the gutter. At least 12 inches of the ladder should extend above the gutter to provide safe working conditions.

First block the gutter outlet with a rag. Then, wearing heavy work gloves to avoid cuts, remove debris from the gutters. Scrape accumulated silt into a heap using a shaped piece of plastic or light sheetmetal. Then scoop it out with a garden trowel and deposit it in a bucket hung from the ladder.

Sweep the gutter with a whisk broom, then remove the rag and flush the gutter using a garden hose. Check whether the water drains completely; standing pools indicate a sagging gutter section.

Seal leaking seams where gutter sections are joined with silicone caulk. For the best seal, disassemble the sections, apply caulk inside the seam, then reassemble. Or spread caulk over the seam on the inside of the gutter and smooth the surface to avoid producing water-trapping ridges.

If downspouts are clogged, free them using a plumber's snake or drain auger. Work from the bottom if possible, to avoid compacting debris further. If necessary, disassemble the downspout sections to get at the blockage.

If downspout blockages are frequent, install leaf strainers in the gutter outlets. Or in severe situations, attach wire-mesh leaf guards over the entire length of the gutters to slow the accumulation of debris.

Leaf strainer   **Wire-mesh leaf guard**

Snow and ice

Gutters can be badly distorted and even broken when large amounts of snow and ice accumulate inside. Dislodge the buildup with a broom from an upstairs window—if you can reach it safely. Otherwise, climb a ladder to clean the gutter.

If snow and ice become a regular seasonal problem, you should screw a snow board to the roof. Make it out of 1 x 3 lumber treated with a wood preservative. Install it about 1 inch above the eaves, using steel straps as shown on the right.

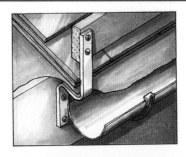

A snow board protects gutters from snow and ice

Building codes

Building codes are comprehensive guidelines intended to set standards for construction practices and material specifications. Their purpose is to ensure the adequate structural and mechanical performance, fire safety, and overall quality of buildings. They are also designed to address various health and environmental concerns related to how buildings are constructed. By setting minimum standards, building codes also limit unfair competitive practices between builders and between contractors.

Building codes address nearly every detail of building construction, from the acceptable recipes for concrete used in the foundation to the permissible fire rating of the roof finish material. Partly because codes attempt to be as comprehensive as possible, and also because they must address different concerns in different parts of the country, they are very detailed, complex, and lack uniformity from one region to another. A further complication is that many new building products become available each year that are not dealt with in the existing codes. Model codes, developed by four major organizations, are widely used for reference throughout the United States.

The Uniform Building Code, published by the International Conference of Building Officials, is very widely accepted. ICBO republishes the entire code every three years and comes out with revisions annually. A short form of the Uniform Building Code is available that covers buildings that are less than three stories high and have fewer than 6000 square feet of living space. This publication was designed for the convenience of most builders and remodelers.

The BOCA Basic Building Code, issued by the Building Officials and Code Administrators International is another widely used code. This code also comes in abridged form for residential construction.

A third model code, prepared by the American Insurance Association, and known as the National Building Code, serves as the basis for many codes that are adopted by local communities. It too is available in short form for matters relating only to home construction.

The Standard Building Code is published by the Southern Building Code Congress International. It addresses conditions and problems that are prevalent in the southern United States.

While it's likely that one of these model codes serves as the basis for the building code in your community, municipal and state governments frequently add standards and restrictions that are not in the model codes. It is your local building department that ultimately decides what is acceptable and what is not. Consult your building department for questions about any code issues. And keep in mind that building codes are primarily designed for the safety of the building's occupants and the general welfare of the community at large. It makes sense to follow all the practices outlined by the code in your area.

Building permits

A building permit is generally required for new construction, remodeling projects that require structural changes or additions, and major demolition projects. In some areas, it's necessary to obtain a building permit for constructing an in-ground pool. In others, you even need a permit to erect scaffolding for painting your house.

To get a building permit, you must file an application (provided by your local building department) that answers questions about the proposed site and the project you are planning. You also have to file a complete set of drawings for the entire project along with detailed specifications for all the mechanical systems. A complete set normally includes a site plan, a foundation plan, a plan for each floor of the house, section views of the house framing from the ridge to the foundation, elevation drawings of all four sides of the house, and drawings for all the mechanical systems. Permit fees are usually based on a percentage of construction costs, or the numbers of trips that the inspector is likely to make to the job site, or both.

At the time you apply for a building permit, ask about other permits that may be required. For example, you may need to apply to the local health department for projects that have an impact on sewage facilities or water supply systems. It's important to arrange inspections in a timely fashion, since each ensuing stage cannot proceed until the previous work has been inspected and approved.

Anyone can file for a building permit, but if you've hired an architect or builder to handle the construction management for you, they should file for all necessary permits.

Zoning restrictions

Even for projects that do not require a building permit, local zoning regulations may limit the scope and nature of the construction that's permitted. Whereas building codes relate to the building itself, zoning rules address the needs and conditions of the community as a whole by regulating the development and uses of the property. Zoning restrictions may apply to situations such as whether a single-family house can be remodeled into apartments, whether a commercial space can be converted into residential use, or the permissible height of a house or outbuilding.

It's a good idea to check with the local zoning board before making any plans, especially plans that substantially change the way the property is used. If planned changes do not conform to existing zoning guidelines, you can apply to the zoning board for a variance. If the board thinks your plans follow the spirit of the regulations, they can approve the changes.

Will you need a permit?

Type of work	Permit required		Zoning approval required	
Interior and exterior painting and minor repairs	NO	Permit may be required to erect scaffolding	NO	Unless in historic district.
Replacing windows and doors	NO		NO	Unless in historic district.
Electrical work	YES	Must be inspected.	NO	Some outdoor lighting may be subject to approval.
Plumbing	YES		NO	Work involving water supply or sewage system may require health department approval.
Heating	NO		NO	
Constructing patios and decks Installing a hot tub	NO		NO	
Structural alterations	YES		NO	Unless house is in an historic district.
Attic conversion	NO YES	No, if work is minor like adding a simple bedroom. Yes, if major structural work is done and if plumbing and major electrical modifications are called for.	NO	Unless work impacts exterior of house in historic district.
Building a fence or garden wall	NO		YES	In cases where a fence or wall is adjacent to a public road, there may be height restrictions.
Planting a hedge	NO	Unless it obscures the view of traffic at a junction, or access to a main road.	NO	
Path or sidewalk	NO	Unless it will be used by the public.	NO	Unless in historic district.
Clearing land	NO		YES	
Installing a satellite-TV dish	NO		NO	
Constructing a small outbuilding	YES	Local codes usually have size restrictions. Anything smaller doesn't need a permit.	NO	Unless in historic district.
Porch addition	YES	Local codes sometimes have size limits. Under the limit doesn't require permit.	NO	Unless in historic district.
Greenhouse or sunspace	YES		NO	Unless in historic district.
Building a garage	YES		YES	If used for a commercial vehicle or located close to property line.
Driveway paving	NO		YES	At point where it meets the road.
House addition	YES		NO	Unless house is in historic district or addition will be close to property line.
Demolition	YES	If major work is done that involves any structural elements.	NO	Unless house is in historic district.
Converting single-family house into apartments	YES		YES	
Converting residential building to commercial use	YES		YES	

CHART
Building code requirements and zoning regulations vary from town to town and frequently have county and state restrictions added to them. For this reason, it's impossible to state with certainty which home-improvement projects require official permission and which do not. This chart lists some of the most frequently undertaken projects and is meant to serve as a rough guide only. Taken as a whole, it suggests a certain logic for anticipating what type of approval may be needed. Whether or not official approval is required, all work should be carried out to the standards established in local codes.

BUILDER'S TOOLS

A specialist builder—such as a plasterer, finish carpenter, or bricklayer—needs only a limited set of tools, whereas the amateur is more like a one-man general builder who has to be able to tackle all kinds of construction and repair work, and therefore requires a much wider range of tools than the specialist.

The selection suggested here is for renovating and improving the structure of your home and for such tasks as building or restoring garden structures and laying paving. Electrical work, decorating, and plumbing call for other sets of tools.

FLOATS AND TROWELS

For a professional builder, floats and trowels have their specific uses, but in home maintenance a repointing trowel may often be the ideal tool for patching small areas of plaster, or a plasterer's trowel for smoothing concrete.

Using a mortar hawk
A mortar hawk makes tuckpointing mortar joints very easy. Place the lip of the hawk just under a horizontal joint and scrape the mortar into place with a jointer or pointing trowel.

● **Essential tools**
Brick trowel
Pointing trowel
Plasterer's trowel
Mortarboard
Hawk
Spirit level
Try square
Plumb line

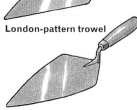

London-pattern trowel

Canadian-pattern trowel

Brick and block trowels

A brick or block trowel is for handling and placing mortar when laying bricks or concrete blocks. A professional might use one with a blade as long as 1 foot, but such a trowel is too heavy and unwieldy for the amateur.

The blade of a **London-pattern trowel** has one curved edge for cutting bricks, a skill that takes practice to perfect; the blade's other edge is straight, for picking up mortar. You can buy left-handed versions of this trowel or opt for a similar trowel with two straight edges.

A **Canadian-pattern trowel** (sometimes called a Philadelphia brick trowel) is also symmetrical, having a wide blade with two curved edges.

Pointing trowel

A pointing trowel is designed for repairing and shaping mortar joints between bricks. The blade is only 3 to 4 inches long.

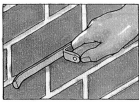

Jointer

Use a jointer to shape the mortar joints between bricks. Its narrow blade is dragged along the mortar joint, and the curved front end is used for shaping the verticals.

Wooden float

A wooden float is for applying and smoothing concrete to a fine, attractive texture. The more expensive ones have detachable handles, so their wooden blades can be replaced when they wear out. Similar floats made from plastic are also available.

Plasterer's trowel

A plasterer's trowel is a steel float for applying plaster and cement renderings to walls. It is also dampened and used for "polishing"—smoothing the surface of the material when it has firmed up. Some builders prefer to apply stucco with a heavy trowel and finish it with a more flexible blade, but you need to be quite skilled to exploit such subtle differences.

BOARDS FOR CARRYING MORTAR OR PLASTER

Any conveniently sized sheet of ½- or ¾-inch exterior-grade plywood can be used as a mixing board for plaster or mortar. A panel about 3 feet square makes an ideal mixing board, while a smaller board, about 2 feet square, is convenient for carrying the material to the work site. Screwing battens to the underside of either board makes it easier to lift and carry.

You will also need a small lightweight hawk for carrying pointing mortar or plaster. Make one by nailing a block of wood underneath a plywood board so that you can plug a handle into it.

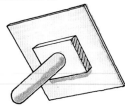

A homemade hawk

LEVELING AND MEASURING TOOLS

You can make some leveling and measuring tools yourself—but don't skimp on essentials, such as a good spirit level and a robust tape measure.

VIAL

Spirit level

A spirit level is a machine-made straightedge incorporating special glass tubes or vials that contain a liquid. In each vial an air bubble floats. When a bubble rests exactly between two lines marked on the glass, that indicates that the structure on which the level is held is precisely horizontal or vertical, depending on the orientation of the vial.

Buy a wooden or lightweight aluminum level, 2 to 3 feet long. A well-made one is very strong, but treat it with care and always clean mortar or plaster from it before it sets.

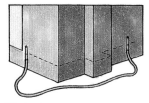

Water level

You can make a water level by plugging short lengths of transparent plastic tubing into the two ends of a garden hose; fill the hose with water until it appears in both tubes. Since water level remains constant, the levels in the tubes are always identical and so can be used for marking identical heights, even over long distances and round obstacles and bends.

Builder's square

A large square is useful when setting out brick or concrete-block corners. The best squares are stamped out of sheetmetal, but you can make a serviceable one by cutting out a right-angle triangle from thick plywood with a hypotenuse of about 2 feet 6 inches. Cut out the center of the triangle to reduce the weight.

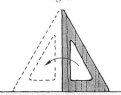

Checking a square

Accuracy is important, so check the square by placing it against a perfectly straight board on the floor. Draw a line against the square to make a right angle with the board, then flop the square to see if it forms the same angle from the other side.

Try square

Use a try square for marking out square cuts or joints on lumber.

Tape measure
An ordinary retractable steel tape measure is adequate for most purposes; but if you need to measure a large plot, buy a wind-up tape, 50 to 100 feet in length.

Making a plumb line
Any small, heavy weight hung on a length of fine string can act as a plumb line for judging whether a structure or surface is vertical.

Bricklayer's line
This is a nylon line used as a guide for laying bricks or blocks level. It is stretched between two flat-bladed pins, which are driven into vertical joints at the ends of a wall or between line blocks that hook over the bricks at the ends of a course. As a substitute, you can stretch string between two stakes driven into the ground outside the line of the wall.

Steel pins and line
You can buy special flat-bladed pins to hold a line that guides in laying a straight course of bricks.

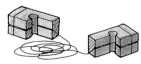

Line blocks
The blocks grip the corners of the bricks or blocks at the end of a course; the line passes through their slots.

Straightedge
Any length of straight rigid lumber can be used to check whether a surface is flat or, in conjunction with a spirit level, to see whether two points are at the same height.

Story pole
For gauging the height of brick courses, calibrate a softwood batten by making saw cuts across it at intervals equal to the thickness of a brick plus one mortar joint. Blocks of wood at each end enable a story pole to span irregularities.

Marking gauge
A marking gauge has a sharp steel point for scoring a line on lumber parallel to the edge. It has an adjustable fence that keeps the point a constant distance from the edge.

HAMMERS
Several types of hammer are useful on a building site.

Claw hammer
Choose a strong claw hammer for building stud walls, nailing floorboards, making door frames and window frames, and putting up garden fencing.

Hand sledge
A heavy hand sledge is used for driving cold chisels and for a variety of demolition jobs. It is also useful for driving large masonry nails into walls.

Sledgehammer
Buy a sledgehammer if you have to break up concrete or masonry. It's also the best tool for driving stakes or fence posts into the ground, though you can make do with a hand sledge if the ground is not too hard.

Mallet
A wooden carpenter's mallet is the proper tool for driving a wood chisel. But you can use a metal hammer instead if the chisel has an impact-resistant plastic handle.

SAWS
Every builder needs a range of handsaws, but consider buying a circular saw when you have to cut a lot of heavy structural lumber—especially if you have a lot of ripping to do, which is a very tiring job when done by hand.

Special saws are available for cutting metal and even for sawing through masonry.

Panel saw
All kinds of manufactured panels are used in house construction, so it is worth investing in a good panel saw.

It can also be used for cutting large structural lumber to the required lengths.

General-purpose saw
A single handsaw that can be used equally well for ripping solid planks lengthwise and crosscutting them to size is a useful tool to have on a building site. A saw with hardened teeth is also an asset.

Backsaw
This is a good saw for accurately cutting small pieces of trim, paneling, and joints. The metal stiffening along the top of the blade keeps it rigid and prevents the saw from wandering off line.

Keyhole saw
This small saw has a narrow tapered blade for cutting holes in lumber and panel stock.

Coping saw
A coping saw has a frame that holds a fairly coarse but very narrow blade under tension for cutting curves in wood.

Floorboard saw
If you pry a floorboard above its neighbors, you can cut across it with an ordinary tenon saw, but the curved cutting edge of a floorboard saw makes it easier to avoid damaging the boards on either side.

Hacksaw
The hardened-steel blades of a hacksaw have fine teeth for cutting metal. Use one to cut steel concrete-reinforcing rods or small pieces of sheetmetal.

All-purpose saw
An all-purpose saw is able to cut wood, metal, plastics, and building boards. The short frameless blade has a low-friction coating.

This type of saw is especially useful for cutting scrap lumber, which may contain nails or screws that would dull the blade of an ordinary saw.

Circular saw
A circular saw will quickly and accurately rip lumber or manufactured panels down to size. As well as saving you the effort of handsawing large stock, a sharp power saw produces such a clean cut that there is often no need for planing afterward. If your preference is for a cordless circular saw, buy a spare battery and keep it charged.

Reciprocating saw
A reciprocating saw is a two-handed power saw that has a long pointed blade. It is powerful enough to saw sections of heavy lumber, and can even cut through a complete stud wall. With a change of blade, you can use a reciprocating saw to cut metal pipes. Both cordless and corded versions are available.

Gas-engine masonry saw
A gas-engine masonry saw is strictly a rental item. Still, there is no substitute for one when it comes to masonry demolition.

● **Essential tools**
Straightedge
Tape measure
Claw hammer
Hand sledge
Panel saw
Tenon saw
Hacksaw
Keyhole saw
Power jigsaw
Power drill
Masonry bits
Brace and bits

Drilling masonry for wall plugs
Set the drill to hammer action and low speed. Wrap tape around the bit to mark the depth to be drilled, allowing for slightly more depth than the length of the plug, as dust will pack down into the hole as the plug is inserted. Drill the hole in stages, partly withdrawing the bit at times to clear the debris.

To protect paintwork and floor coverings from falling dust, tape a paper bag just below the position of the hole before drilling.

Builder's tools

● **Essential tools**
Glass cutter
Putty knife
Cold chisel
Brick chisel
Spade
Shovel
Rake
Wheelbarrow
Cabinet screwdriver
Phillips-head
 screwdriver
Jack plane

DRILLS

A powerful electric drill is invaluable to a builder. A cordless version is useful when you have to bore holes outdoors or in attics and cellars that lack convenient electrical outlets.

Power drill

Buy a good-quality power drill, plus a range of twist drills and spade or power-bore bits for drilling wood. Make sure the drill has a percussion or hammer action for drilling masonry walls. For masonry you need special drill bits tipped with tungsten carbide. The smaller ones are matched to the size of standard wall plugs; there are also much larger ones that have reduced shanks, so they can be used in a standard drill chuck.

Brace

A brace is the ideal hand tool for drilling large holes in lumber. In addition, when fitted with a screwdriver bit, it provides the necessary power for driving or removing large woodscrews.

GLAZIER'S TOOLS

Glass is such a hard and brittle material that it can only be worked with specialized tools.

Glass cutter

A glass cutter does not actually cut glass but merely scores a line in it. This is done by a tiny hardened-steel wheel or a chip of industrial diamond mounted in a penlike holder. The glass breaks along the scored line when pressure is applied to it.

Beam-compass cutter

A beam-compass cutter is for scoring circles on glass that enable you to either cut a round hole or create a circular pane. The cutting wheel is mounted at the end of an adjustable beam that turns on a central pivot that's attached to the glass by a suction cup.

Crowbar

A crowbar, or wrecking bar, is used for demolishing lumber framework. Force the flat tip between the components and use the leverage of the long shaft to pry them apart. Choose a crowbar that has a claw at one end for removing large nails.

Slater's ripper

To replace individual slates or wooden shingles you must cut their fixing nails without disturbing the pieces overlapping them, and for this you need a slater's ripper. Pass the long hooked blade up between the shingles, locate one of the hooks over the fixing nail, and pull down sharply to cut it.

Spear-point glass drill

A glass drill has a flat tungsten-steel tip shaped like a spearhead. The shape of the tip is designed to reduce friction that would otherwise crack the glass, but it does need lubricating with oil or water during drilling.

Hacking knife

A hacking knife is often a shop-made tool with a heavy steel blade for chipping old putty out of window rabbets in order to remove the glass. To use it, place the point between the putty and the frame, then tap the back of the blade with a hammer.

Putty knife

The blade of a putty knife is used for shaping and smoothing fresh putty when reglazing a window. You can choose between a chisel type with a thick, stiff blade, or a standard putty knife with a thin, flexible blade. Putty knives are also useful for removing paint and other light-duty scraping jobs.

CHISELS

As well as chisels for cutting and paring wood joints, you'll need some special ones when you are working on masonry.

Cold chisel

Cold chisels are made from solid-steel-hexagonal-section rod. They are primarily for cutting metal bars and chopping the heads off rivets, but a builder will use one for cutting a notch in brickwork or for chopping hardware embedded in brick.
Slip a plastic safety sleeve over the chisel to protect your hand from a misplaced blow with a hammer.

Plugging chisel

A plugging chisel has a narrow, flat tip for cutting out old or eroded pointing. It's worth having when you have a large area of brickwork to repoint.

Brick chisel

The wide blade of a brick chisel is designed for cutting bricks and concrete blocks. It is also useful for other heavy chopping and prying jobs.

WORK GLOVES

Wear strong work gloves whenever you are carrying paving rubble, concrete blocks, or rough lumber. Ordinary gardening gloves are better than none, but they won't last very long on a building site. The best work gloves have leather palms and fingers, although you may prefer a pair with ventilated backs for comfort in hot weather.

DIGGING TOOLS

Much building work requires some kind of digging. You probably have the basic tools in your garden shed; the others you can rent.

Pickax

Use a medium-weight pickax to break up heavily compacted soil—especially if it contains a lot of buried rubble.

Spade

Buy a good-quality spade for excavating soil and mixing concrete. One with a stainless-steel blade is best, but alloy steel lasts reasonably well. Choose a strong hardwood or reinforced fiberglass shaft with a D-shaped handle that's riveted with metal plates on its crosspiece. Make sure the hollow shaft socket and blade are forged in one piece.

Shovel

You can use a spade for mixing and placing concrete or mortar, but the raised edges of a shovel retain it better.

Wheelbarrow

Most garden wheelbarrows are not strong enough for construction, which generally involves carting heavy loads of rubble and wet concrete. Unless the tubular underframe of the wheelbarrow is rigidly braced, the wheelbarrow's thin metal body will distort and may well spill its load as you are crossing rough ground.
 Check, too, that the axle is fastened securely—a cheap wheelbarrow can lose its wheel as you are tipping a load into place.

SCREWDRIVERS

Most people gradually acquire an assortment of screwdrivers over a period of time, as and when the need arises. Alternatively, buy a power screwdriver with a range of bits or buy screwdriver bits for your power drill.

Cabinet screwdriver

Buy at least one large flat-tip screwdriver. The fixed variety is quite adequate, but a pump-action one, which drives large screws very quickly, is useful when assembling large projects.

Phillips-head screwdriver

Choose the size and type of Phillips-head screwdriver to suit the work at hand. There is no "most-useful size," as each driver must fit a screw slot exactly.

PLANES

Furniture building may call for molding or grooving planes, but most household joinery needs only a light pass to remove saw marks and leave a fairly smooth finish.

Jack plane

A jack plane is a medium-size bench plane; it's the most versatile general-purpose tool.

Glossary

B

Baluster
One of a set of vertical posts supporting a stair handrail.

Balustrade
A handrail along the top of the balusters (posts) on a staircase or landing.

Banister
A balustrade, a handrail along a staircase.

Batt
A flat, insulating filler, as of fiberglass or mineral fiber.

Batten
A narrow strip of wood.

Blind nailing
A nailing technique that leaves no visible nailhead on the surface of the workpiece. Nails are driven at an angle.

Blocking
A short piece of wood between studs or joists, providing extra strength to a framework.

Brown coat
The middle layer of stucco, applied after the first, or scratch, coat and before the finish coat.

C

Casing
The wooden molding around a door or window opening.

Cavity wall
A wall of two separate masonry skins with an air space between them.

Chamfer
A narrow, flat surface on the edge of a workpiece, normally at a 45-degree angle to adjacent surfaces. Also, to plane the angled surface.

Cornice
The decorative molding course between walls and ceiling.

Counterbore
To cut a hole that allows the head of a bolt or screw to lie below a surface. Also, the hole itself.

Countersink
To cut a tapered recess that allows the head of a screw to lie flush with a surface. Also, the tapered recess itself.

Course
A continuous layer of bricks, masonry, tiles, or other wallcovering.

Cove molding
A decorative molding with a concave section or with a trough for hidden lighting.

Cowl
A chimney covering that helps to control airflow.

Creosote
A flammable, tarry substance, exuded from burning wood, that forms on the inside walls of chimneys.

D

Dado
A groove cut into a piece of wood to make a joint, running across the grain.

Damp-proof course
A layer of impervious material that prevents moisture from rising through the ground into the walls of a masonry building.

Deadmen
A T-shaped brace used to support workpieces, such as drywall, on a ceiling during installation.

Dormer
A vertical window projecting from a sloping roof.

Drip groove
A groove cut or molded in the underside of a door or windowsill to prevent rainwater from running back to the wall.

E

Eaves
The lower edge of a sloping roof that project beyond the walls.

Extension
A length of electrical cable for temporarily connecting an appliance to a wall socket. Also, a structural addition to an existing building.

F

Fascia board
Strip of wood that covers the ends of rafters and to which gutters are attached.

Flashing
A weatherproof junction between a roof and a wall or chimney, or between one roof and another.

Flue
The chimney pipe or other passageway that carries smoke to the outer air.

Footing
A narrow concrete foundation for a wall.

Furring strips
Parallel strips of wood fixed to a wall or ceiling to provide a framework for attaching panels.

G

Gable roof
Two sloping roofs joined at a center ridge, forming a triangular shape.

Gambrel roof
A roof with the slope broken into two different pitches, generally one at a sharper and one at a shallower angle.

Galvanized
Covered with a protective coating of zinc.

Glazier
A glassworker.

Glazing
Architectural glasswork, glass windows, or doors.

Gypsum
A mineral material used in drywall.

H

Header
The top horizontal member of a wooden frame.

Hip roof
A roof with four sides, all sloping up to the center.

I

I-beam
An I-shaped steel supporting beam.

J

Jack studs
Shorter studs that support headers.

Jalousie
A window with horizontal glass louvers that adjust to allow airflow.

Jamb
A vertical upright that forms the side of an opening, or the framework of the opening as a whole.

Joist
A horizontal wooden beam used to support a floor or ceiling.

K

Key, keyed, keying
To prepare a surface by abrading it so that coatings such as glue or plaster will adhere.

L

Lath
Narrow strips of material nailed to walls, joists, etc., to provide support for plaster.

Lintel
A loadbearing horizontal member above an opening, such as a door.

Glossary

M

Marine plywood
Plywood meeting specific requirements governing continuing immersion in water.

Miter
A joint formed between two workpieces by cutting bevels of equal angles at the ends of each piece. Also, to cut such a joint.

Mortise
A slot cut in lumber or other material to receive a matching tongue or tenon.

Mullion
A thin, vertical divider between panes of a window or door.

Muntin
A central vertical member of a panel door.

N

Newel
A decorative vertical post supporting the handrail on a staircase or landing.

Nosing
The front edge of a stair tread.

P

Parge
To coat with plaster.

Pilot hole
A small-diameter hole drilled when setting a woodscrew to act as a guide for the screw's thread.

Plaster of paris
A powder mixed with water to make a paste for molded plasterwork and repairs.

Pointing
To form the mortar joints binding bricks together.

Primer
The first coat of a paint system, serving to protect the workpiece and reduce absorption of subsequent coats.

Purlin
A horizontal beam that provides intermediate support for rafters or sheet roofing.

R

Radius
The measurement of a circle by a line from the center to the circumference of the circle.

Rafter
One of a set of parallel sloping beams that form the main structural element of a roof.

Riser
The vertical part of a step. Also, a pipe that supplies water, by pressure, to upward locations.

Run
The horizontal measurement between the top and bottom risers of a stair or the depth of one tread.

S

Sash
The framework holding the panes of the window. Also, the whole operable part of the window.

Scratch coat
The bottom, or first, layer of stucco.

Screed
A thin layer of mortar applied to give a smooth surface to concrete or other mortar. Also, to smooth a concrete surface until it is flat.

Scribe
To mark or score a guiding line on a surface.

Sheathing
The outer layer of insulation surrounding electrical cable. Also, the outer covering of a stud-framed wall that is applied beneath the wall siding.

Sill
The lowest horizontal member of a stud partition. Also, the lowest horizontal member of a door or window frame.

Sleeper wall
A low masonry wall used as an intermediate support for first-floor joists.

Soffit
The underside of a part of a building, such as the eaves or archway.

Sole plate
The sill of a stud partition. Also called bottom plate.

Stile
A vertical side member of a door or window sash.

Stringer
A board that runs from one floor level to another, into that staircase treads and risers are jointed.

Stucco
A thin layer of cement-based mortar applied to walls to provide a protective or decorative finish. Also, to apply the mortar.

Stud partition
An interior stud-framed dividing wall.

Studs
The vertical members of a stud-framed wall.

T

Tempered glass
Glass treated to strengthen it and to cause it to break into pellets rather than shards.

Toenail
To fasten by driving nails in at an angle.

Topcoat
The outer layer of a paint system.

Tread
The horizontal part of a step.

U

Undercoat
A layer or layers of paint used to obliterate the color of a primer and build a protective layer of paint before applying a topcoat.

V

Vanes
The vertical panels or slats on vertical window and door blinds.

Vapor barrier
A layer of impervious material that prevents the passage of moisture-laden air.

W

Wall angle
A metal angled piece, such as an angle iron, used to fasten two surfaces at a joint, as for fixing a suspended ceiling system to walls.

Wall plate
A horizontal member placed along the top of a wall to support the ends of joists and spread their load.

Wall tie
A usually metal piece used to reinforce joints in brickwork and masonry.

Weather strip
Thin strips of various materials set around structural openings to keep out the weather.

Winders
Tapered treads on a circular or curving staircase, in which one end of the tread is wider than the other.

Index